EXIT THE MAZE

EXIT THE MAZE

→

One Addiction, One Cause, One Solution

DR. DONNA MARKS

BEYOND WORDS

Portland, Oregon

BEYOND WORDS

1750 S.W. Skyline Blvd, Suite 20
Portland, Oregon 97221-2543
503-531-8700 / 503-531-8773 fax
www.beyondword.com

First Beyond Words paperback edition November 2022
Previously published by Westward Publishing in 2020, ISBN: 978-0-578-59545-0

BEYOND WORDS PUBLISHING is an imprint of Simon & Schuster, Inc., and the Beyond Words logo is a registered trademark of Beyond Words Publishing, Inc.

For information about special discounts for bulk purchases, please contact Beyond Words Special Sales at 503-531-8700 or specialsales@beyondword.com.

Managing editor: Lindsay S. Easterbrooks-Brown
Editors: Michele Ashtiani Cohn, Bailey Potter
Copyeditor: Gretchen Stelter
Proofreader: Linda M. Meyer
Design: Devon Smith
Composition: William H. Brunson Typography Services

Manufactured in the United States of America

10 9 8 7 6 5 4 3 2 1

Library of Congress Control Number: 2022946060

ISBN 978-1-58270-894-2
ISBN 978-1-58270-895-9 (ebook)

The corporate mission of Beyond Words Publishing, Inc.: *Inspire to Integrity*

*This book is dedicated to anyone who feels lost, stuck in a maze,
and is ready to return to the love that you are
and the life you were meant to have.*

CONTENTS

FOREWORD

I first met Donna Marks over thirty years ago, when we were active in an organization that advocated for mental health counselors and their patients. Our initial bonding centered on our mutual frustration that our training did not prepare us for certain types of patients. We could effectively help people who were having difficulty adjusting to a loss or a life change, but we could not help severely traumatized people who'd either split off from reality—literally—or escaped altogether through substance abuse. It didn't take long to discover that most of these patients were labeled "untreatable," but we were determined to get the answers our souls demanded. During the next thirty years, though our paths rarely crossed, we independently dug deeper into the few resources available that could give us the tools to best help our patients fully recover and be restored to the lives they deserved to have.

Eventually, fate brought us back to working together on those challenging cases, except now we enjoy the fruits of success, instead of utter madness of frustration. It's ultimately up to the patient to want to heal more than they want anything else, but unlike before, now we can carry the lantern and guide them to restoration and wholeness.

Exit the Maze: One Addiction, One Cause, One Solution is the summation of Dr. Marks's journey through the successes and failures that propelled her quest for healing. She was determined to ignore the naysayers and stood firm on her findings about why addiction treatment succeeded or failed. *Exit the Maze* is explosive, and it deserves to be celebrated. Marks explores the emotional emptiness that underlies addiction for most patients. Marks's journey forced her to face that void in herself that never allowed her to feel authentic or fully recover, despite following the many suggestions made by her therapists and advisors. The book is rich with her worldwide research and documentation of this pandemic-level problem and its impact on our physical and mental health. In addition, it is replete with hard-earned personal and professional insights—straightforward, honest, gutsy, and passed on to all of us in plain, simple terms.

Dr. Marks confronts the truth and does not hesitate to call out a failing treatment system that has lost its way when treating addiction. Alcoholics Anonymous and Narcotics Anonymous do one thing exquisitely: stop the use of whatever substance is being used. However, the ability to stop or even retard the underlying causes fails miserably. As pointed out in this book, national research models report a small success rate. *Exit the Maze* does not focus on the many addicts who have received successful treatment. Marks's focus is on the significantly greater number of addicts that relapse with little to no recovery success.

Marks also changes the narrative that addicts are at the bottom rung of the social ladder and reports the facts about the many people who (knowingly or unknowingly) suffer all kinds of addiction. Marks has substantiated the claim that a nation consumed with denial and a plethora of incomplete and uncoordinated definitions of addiction leaves the door open for convoluted treatment destined to fail. Programs are not treating the causes of anxiety and depression, eating disorders, attention-deficit disorder, bipolar disorder, posttraumatic stress disorder, obsessive-compulsive disorder, and dissociative disorders, all of which are found in the addiction community. Instead, they medicate these symptoms and avoid any pain caused by the family of origin issues. Marks believes that family treatment should correlate with the addict's so that the family can heal together. Treatment could address the childhood trauma (if any), as well as the trauma that addiction has caused the family.

It is critical to face the relationship between these mental health issues and addiction and how commonly there is a misdiagnosis. Frequently, by the time an addict gets diagnosed, they've received multiple diagnoses from different mental health professionals and tried various medications without successful remission. It's true. The symptoms of addiction and mental health illnesses are often similar: anxiety, depression, psychosis, mania, but a skilled clinician deciphers the causes. Are the symptoms due to addiction, or is there an organic brain disorder? It's hard for me to believe that clinicians still fail to make an accurate diagnosis in this current era of mental health treatment.

Supported by years of her own personal recovery and her relentless commitment to education and professional training, Dr. Marks has identified the adverse outcomes of current alcohol and drug treatment models—repeated relapse. Unfortunately, those most responsible for the current treatment approach are resistant to changes to this long-standing approach. This underserves millions of patients and their families. This total focus on a symptoms-only outcome is not working.

Dr. Marks is a breath of fresh air filled with truth and evidence that will create significant, positive changes to patient outcomes. She calls the current models "the treatment trap," which includes unwarranted medication, insufficient counseling, and unwillingness to explore other modalities. To continue the same treatment approach over and over again and expect better results is not insane; it's irrational, irresponsible, and borders on stupidity.

Failure in the addiction treatment industry is the proverbial "elephant in the room," as Marks points out, and the costs to human lives and the billions of dollars wasted should no longer be ignored. Treatment does not embrace the reality of breaking free (out of the maze)—it merely creates an adjacent maze.

Treatment centers focus on the one symptom (alcohol abuse, codependency, drug abuse, gambling, sex addiction, smoking, and so forth) rather than the fact that there's only one addiction. Marks refers to the one addiction as the "invisible hole," a feeling that something is always missing, and it drives the constant search for the next fix. Once a person stops smoking, they switch to eating, a cocaine addict switches to gambling, and so on. Hence the merry-go-round keeps spinning. The concept that you just need to stop a particular addiction and you'll be fine is absurd.

The way out of this maze, according to Marks, is to stop being singularly focused on "trying to get free" and instead to focus on the debilitating emotional, physical, spiritual, and mental damages to a person's soul. Find the root causes in your life that initiated a sense of futility, personal shame, and the loss of hope and self that led to the first-time abuse. By spending more time on the solutions and less time on the drug of choice, you can begin to reclaim power over your mind.

The disease model forces patients to spend more time on recovery than on wellness, constantly trying to keep people from using again rather than moving forward with their lives. The concept of continually referring to oneself as "recovering" is not empowering; it's debilitating, and this false concept never goes away. Fear is rampant in the recovery industry—the fear that if, for one moment, one stops defining themself as an addict, something perilous might happen: relapse.

Exit the Maze is an excellent metaphor for the futility of the addiction treatment industry, which, by its very nature has no way out. Patients are forever caught in that futility. Over the years, I've witnessed thousands of recovering people who are stuck in the "you're never cured" mentality. The best they can hope for is to remain abstinent despite the promise in 12-step meetings to be "happy, joyous, and free."

Powerlessness is an outdated metaphor. To say that recovering person is powerless is not entirely accurate. It's only valid when a person is using. After detox, they are free to do the work that will help them exit the addiction maze forever. However, they must face the causes that formed that initial internal void—this part they are not powerless over.

Treatment often includes all kinds of "healthy" coping skills like yoga, meditation, mindfulness, affirmations, and cognitive therapy. These are all good tools, but they too can become another addiction. Plus, once the patient leaves treatment, they've simply put band-aids on bullet holes. Those wounds continue to fester and push the person back into relapse.

Exit the Maze is ready to be discovered, equal to *Trauma and Recovery*, by Judith Herman, MD, which helped open the treatment door for victims of trauma and abuse. Of course, no one gets well without addressing their underlying (often repressed) mental health issues. Even when we manage the unresolved pain, we're still not there. For example, people who abuse themselves with substances or any other addiction have never learned how to love themselves. And while treatment has come a long way in addressing the underlying causes, we've still a long way to go in helping our patients face and heal those roots.

In chapter 5, Marks lacerates the common notion regarding the birth of addiction. The debate about whether addiction is a genetic disease or a brain disorder is explored. Even if there is a genetic marker, she points out that no gene demands a person ever start drinking alcohol, smoking, using drugs, gambling, drinking caffeine, eating sugar, or any other learned behaviors. It's true that someone with a family history of addiction might correlate to a higher incidence of intergenerational addiction, but it's not absolute. Marks also adamantly disagrees with the theory that addiction is a brain disorder. She doesn't believe that babies are born with addicted brains. Newborns can be dependent if the mother is addicted, but that is not the same as the baby being addicted. She agrees that brain disorder is a part of addiction, but only because the addiction caused the brain to be diseased and not the other way around. Marks believes that as long as we see addiction as a brain disease and continue to treat it with medication, we limit the possibility of a fully recovered brain and a total cure from addiction. Naturally, some people need medication, but it should not be the first protocol. Every person deserves to explore all of the treatment possibilities.

Marks boldly states the truth that emotional and physical trauma lies at the core of addiction. As a trauma therapist for over thirty years, I can attest that this profound and simple truth is valid. So often, children who lack love, safety, or attachment will find anything to numb the pain to fill the emotional vacuum.

People who have been abused have lost their sense of self-worth and experience self-loathing and loss of personal value. It makes sense that they would continue to harm themselves even when they know better. Some types of abuse even include self-cutting, acting out sexually, lack of setting or honoring boundaries, and ongoing poor judgment despite hitting a wall repeatedly. Relapse is just another way to reinforce feelings of worthlessness, even though the addict thinks they are indulging in something desirable; the addiction provides momentary relief from overwhelming pain. As one of my patients put it, "I want to scream until my lungs bleed. I want to scream until my lungs burst out of my chest." This type of psychic damage permeates one's whole being. Until this pain is addressed the odds of repeated relapse are highly likely.

Someone who's not operating as an empty vessel trying to ward off pain is not susceptible to the addictive mindset. People who feel good about themselves can choose healthy attachments and, when confronted with adversities, can regulate their moods without crashing. However, for an addict, bumping up against a conflict is like sticking their finger into an emotional electrical socket. They will do anything to avoid the socket and the subsequent pain. The addict who has no way to soothe themselves is ultimately destined to relapse, and the harsh reality is that this could lead to overdose or even suicide.

There's nothing on the market quite like *Exit the Maze*—clinically sound, well researched, and presented to the reader as a gift of hope. This book is unique because Marks recognizes that abstinence and healing trauma is not enough. The missing link is to replace all pathology with self-love. People have learned to equate love with a feeling they get, thus the constant chase to obtain these desired states. Marks believes that all addictions are a substitute for love, and that we've confused doing something that feels good with the behaviors that make us feel good about ourselves. Once a person fills the internal emptiness with loving behaviors, the desire to get high will be forgotten. Rather than unconsciously continuing to do what only makes them feel good for a short time and worse in the long run, they learn to choose loving behavior instead.

Dr. Marks is right: a war on drugs will never work. Wars are about fighting an enemy, but the only approach when the enemy is on the inside is self-love. The enemy can no longer be the treatment industry itself. Marks implores you to face your fears, transcend them, learn to love yourself, and embrace life. Addiction is not a choice. It's a destructive behavior that controls your life.

It is time to come together and take recovering people across the finish line. I agree with Donna Marks and John Lennon, love is the answer. Addiction is no longer of interest once you learn how to love yourself and love your life. You no longer struggle with what to do or not to do. Being addicted to anything simply loses all value to you.

In conclusion, without reservation, I recommend taking a risk, confronting any resistance, and starting the journey to self-love by reading *Exit the Maze: One Addiction, One Cause, One Solution*. This masterpiece can lead you out of prison and into the freedom you are meant to have.

—George L. Wallace-Barnhill, PhD,
author of *The Jukebox of Life*

INTRODUCTION

THE ADDICTION MAZE

A rat in a maze is free to go anywhere,
as long as it stays inside the maze.
—Margaret Atwood, *The Handmaid's Tale*

When we think of a maze, most of us think of a fun puzzle we did as children. It had an entrance and an exit, and the only goal was to find your way out. You'd draw a line through a series of corridors to find the exit, which often was located at the perimeter, on the opposite side of the maze from the entrance. Your pencil line might have hit a few dead ends, and you might even have become a little frustrated, but through trial and error, you'd learn to see the paths that didn't work and find your way through.

Another type of maze is one I encountered in a psychology class. We used the maze to test the behavior of mice and how they learn. These mazes were three-dimensional, so the dead ends were walls, not just lines on paper. Research scientists would do experiments with mice in mazes that included rewards such as food or punishments such as a mild electric current. In some cases, the mice would keep hitting a lever to get morphine or would run to-and-fro to get a reward and, depending on how badly they wanted the reward, sometimes do so to the point of pain or exhaustion.

A person operating under addictive behavior is like a mouse looking for cheese in a maze—they frantically run through the maze looking for the cheese, not caring about how big the reward is or the other consequences, such as being shocked. No matter what, they will search for the reward; even if the mouse is traumatized, presented with the opportunity it will still go after that end goal. Obsessed with getting the reward, the mouse never seeks an exit from the maze.

A person caught in the maze of addiction is similar to the mouse in that the addict will continue to seek out the "cheese" (a metaphor for any addictive substance or behavior) in spite of negative feedback, no matter how punishing it becomes. Like the mouse, the addicted person will continue to run the maze, frantically searching for the next "reward" or fix.

This has become a massive social problem.

Although addicts often are shamed for their behavior, addiction is not something to be ashamed of. It is a symptom of a greater problem that the person didn't create. In modern societies, people have been conditioned to take a pill for just about everything. When a person feels anxious or depressed, the doctor prescribes a pill, sometimes in tandem with counseling but often not. In 2017, there were more than forty million adults in the United States diagnosed with anxiety,[1] 280 million adults worldwide who've suffered at least one bout of depression,[2] with increasing numbers since COVID-19,[3] and twenty-five million people in the United States who have taken antidepressants.[4] More than twenty million antidepressants were prescribed between October and December 2020, an increase of 6 percent in one year.[5] Many people have found themselves unable to stop antidepressant use due to side effects such as headaches, dizziness, nausea, and mood swings—the same as for many other addictive drug withdrawals.[6]

Of the thousands of people with whom I have worked, every person has either been addicted or had a family member or loved one who was. I want to change your perception of addiction from "something wrong with the person addicted" to "something that's wrong with our conditioning." We live in a society that unconsciously attempts to replace love with endless substitutes. If you are struggling with addiction, know that you are not alone. You are one of millions who are paying the price for society's lack of love.

More than half of all deaths in the United States are related to heart disease or cancer,[7] often caused by abusing the body through some form of (diagnosed or undiagnosed) addiction. World Health Organization reports that "heart and lung diseases, cancers, and diabetes are the world's largest killers, with an estimated thirty-eight million deaths annually."[8] What we're not understanding is that most of these illnesses are directly related to the repeated use of substances that result in terminal illnesses. One of the main causes of heart disease is obesity. But what causes obesity? Remember, addiction is defined as doing the same thing again and again despite negative consequences. The abuse of alcohol, sugar, drugs, and trans fats are at the root of most of these illnesses and have been consumed to the point of causing permanent damage to the heart, lungs, kidneys, pancreas, and blood vessels.[9] We're repeatedly warned about our "bad habits" but are rarely referred to someplace to learn how to stop. We just keep treating the symptoms—medically, not psychologically. We're missing the mark here.

In the United States alone, well over a hundred million people suffer from addiction. According to the research, there are nearly 15 million alcohol abusers,[10] 9.49 million opiate abusers,[11] ten million with gambling disorders,[12] fifty million addicted to nicotine,[13] seventy million addicted to food,[14] nine million engaged in sex addiction,[15] eighteen million shopping addicts,[16] and 8.1 million have an illegal drug use disorder.[17] If you add up even the few numbers listed here, it represents more than half the U.S. adult population. Note that these numbers do not include those addicted to illegal drugs, video gaming, exercise, work, or any other type of compulsive behavior that can rule a person's life. The type of fix doesn't matter; the brain has one goal: dopamine—the neurotransmitter that creates a sense of pleasure.

Often when I give a public talk, I ask all of the people who have children to raise their hands. I tell them, "If any of you have given your six-month-old baby a cigarette, raise your hand." Of course, no one has raised their hand. Then I ask, "How many of you have given your baby a shot of whiskey? A Valium? A bag of sugar? Six shots of espresso? A little heroin?"

Everyone chuckles, then I ask, "Then why do you suppose you started putting those very things in your own body?"

Dead silence.

The time has come to break that silence and to start answering the question: *Why?* Why are we like mice running in a maze? How did we get here? Why do we stay in the maze? How do we get out?

My Own Journey

I remember one evening when I was about five years old sitting in my animal-print pajamas next to my grandmother watching television. My teddy bear was tucked under one arm while I sucked my thumb on the other hand. A commercial came on that captured my attention. A thin, beautiful woman in a shirtwaist dress leaned against a tree and gazed at her beau. She held a long, slender Salem cigarette, just like the one my grand-mother held in her hand that very moment. That ad branded in my mind that menthol cigarettes were the source of serenity and romance.

It didn't stop there. I drank the sugary Kool-Aid that "made playtime more fun," and I wanted the newest doll or anything else that offered the promise of fun and escape. It never occurred to me that I was being pro-grammed to believe that the ugliness I felt, inside and out, could be swept away with those products.

As the level of pain and trauma (from emotional, physical, and sexual abuse) I endured at home increased, I gradually forgot about the other things that had lifted me and filled me with inspiration: ballet, music, swimming, nature, and the little voice inside that helped me understand there was something wrong in my house and that it wasn't me. But it took time to do ballet, music, and swimming. And to hear that little reassuring voice, I needed at least a moment of quiet and a feeling of safety to connect to it. Eventually, my emotional turmoil increased faster than I could cope.

I first entered the addiction maze at age twelve, when I was offered a Salem cigarette at a slumber party. My lungs warned me with a violent cough, but the instantaneous altered state that clicked in my brain over-rode the harm I was doing to my body. I never intended to smoke pack after pack that night, but that's exactly what I did. The subtle emotional numbing and the sudden sense of belonging to a group gave me a feeling of connection I'd never experienced before. The next day, I was alone, and even though my lungs hurt and I felt sick, getting another cigarette was the predominant thought in my mind. Despite the foul odor and horrible aftertaste, I felt compelled to re-experience the calming euphoria that first drag had provided. The nicotine corridor of the maze formed around me and continued to expand over the years. I'd buy cigarettes from a vending machine, steal them from my grandparents' packs, or bum them from a friend; then when confronted, I'd adamantly deny ever smoking. After a few years, realizing my conscience and free will had been hijacked, I would decide to quit every day. But I'd forget to stop, put it off until the next day, or quit for a few days then start again. Twice I stopped for several months, but then after a crisis, I'd smoke "just one," under the illusion that I could stop at that.

When it came to drinking, however, I was careful to limit my intake. After all, I grew up in an alcoholic household and vowed I would never drink like my stepfather, who consumed a couple of cases of beer a day. But over time, my resolve wore thin and I drank with abandon, further losing myself in the maze. After a suicide attempt at age fifteen, I met my first psychiatrist, and like the next three, he knew nothing about addictions or their effects on children. He also prescribed me Valium. Sometimes, I went to school as high as a kite, but nobody seemed to notice.

By age sixteen, I was married with an infant, waitressing, and going to night school to get my high school diploma. By eighteen, I was divorced and living in a roach-infested apartment in a bad part of town, where I survived an assault at knifepoint. From one crisis to the next, I managed to keep going. Amid the chaos, that same inner voice from youth told me I could do better and inspired me to go to college and work my way up. I spent the next twelve years dedicating myself to my education and training to become a therapist. In spite of all that, it wasn't enough to help me heal, because the substances that were affecting my mental health were never addressed.

The alcohol corridor led me to seek other corridors with different mood-altering experiences. It didn't matter what they were, as long as there was the possibility of reliving that first mind-blowing hit of nicotine. Every addict chases that first rush of *aahhhh*, but addiction never delivers. And each attempt to find it again only lures us deeper into the maze for more.

When I was thirty years old, the impact of addiction on my life became untenable, and I had to get out. After my second divorce, I added marijuana and a new on-and-off addictive relationship to my nicotine and alcohol habits. That's when I had another emotional crash. This time, I went to an addiction counselor who referred me to treatment. Relieved of chemical dependency, I thought I was cured. I did not know I remained in the addiction maze.

I unconsciously pursued whatever route would help me escape myself. Workaholism seemed like a good choice because I made money. But I began to make work more important than time with my children and time alone. Love and sex seemed like normal enjoyments, but neither lasted, and I ping-ponged from one failed marriage to the next. Marathon running and long-distance bicycling were good for my health and provided a "natural" high, but if I didn't get that endorphin rush, I suffered the same irritability and moodiness that is present when jonesing during any addiction. Shopping seemed a harmless distraction, except I had no savings. I also became a recovery and spirituality junkie. I'd always get a blip of relief from the latest book or seminar, but the feeling never lasted. There remained an emptiness inside that nothing could fill.

Eventually, I got addicted to getting better. I turned myself inside out with every imaginable form of therapy. Gestalt therapy helped rid me of backed-up rage toward my stepfather. Biofeedback and hypnotherapy taught me how to relax and stay calm. Cognitive therapy helped me remain rational during upsets. Psychoanalysis offered my first chance at a relationship that supported me through buckets of tears, and for the first time, in my forties, I learned how to trust another human being. Each modality helped pieces of me, but the messages were mixed. The mental health counselors didn't understand addiction, the addiction counselors didn't understand mental health, and neither understood my spiritual void. I remained unhealed.

I scoured the globe in search of spiritual guidance. Church felt more like a business than a place to connect, but I tried and tried. I studied the 12 Steps, Buddhism, Christian Science, kabbalah, shamanism, yoga. Most of the so-called spiritual gurus I encountered were charlatans. I paid enormous fees to listen to charismatic jargon and sound effects amid razzle-dazzle lighting only to discover later that these leaders could talk the talk but couldn't walk the walk.

If I'm honest, my relapse began after my third divorce. After being diagnosed with breast cancer and a left-breast mastectomy, I was prescribed oxycodone (often known by its brand name OxyContin), a potent opioid. The pills altered my mood, but I took them only as prescribed (all of them, including refills), and when they ran out, I didn't think about getting more. This gave me a false sense of confidence that I didn't have a problem with pills. Then, about six weeks later, I had to retake the opiates after a skin grafting for an infection that developed in my left breast. Again, I took all the prescribed pills and stopped. As I look back, I can see that my executive functioning (ability to make sound decisions) was impaired. Even though I wasn't addicted, I made some bad decisions that I later regretted.

Over the next few years, every time I got through one crisis, another ensued. My daughter, Hanna, and I had just moved into a new home and barely escaped a fire that started during the middle of the night. Almost all of our belongings were destroyed. During the next three years, the same house and my business went through significant damage from three different hurricanes, followed by another fire in my business and the death of my daughter's father. I tried to have relationships, but it was always with the wrong people. I managed to stay physically sober, but I suffered a soul sickness. It was only a matter of time until I began to question if I had everything backward. What was the point of staying sober when my life only worsened with every passing year? I might as well say screw it and at least have some fun. When my psychotherapist told me I wasn't an alcoholic and my physician boyfriend agreed, that was all the evidence I needed to start drinking again. I don't blame anyone. Perhaps they couldn't face their own demons. Or maybe they simply didn't understand or didn't want to understand addiction. It's not their fault that they weren't better trained to understand that addiction is rarely apparent. It's the silent killer that slowly dissolves a person's free will and consumes them one moment at a time—while the person thinks they're enjoying every moment even though their life is a shambles.

Confused and disillusioned, I walked away from everything—recovery, spirituality, therapy. What was the point in all this work? But it didn't take drinking and drugging for long before I saw the disasters I was creating, especially for my children, who, for twenty-three years, saw a sober mom. I was making stupid decisions and had stopped caring

And then, like the prodigal child, I came back. There had to be a way to live a happy, sober life, and I had to figure it out.

After much contemplation, I recognized that my life was a jumble of many different puzzles with all the pieces thrown together in one giant bag. Now, before I could get well, I had to sit with myself and gather and organize the pieces that created the life I wanted—and to eliminate the rest.

The first piece was sobriety; without that, nothing else could fall into place. I returned to recovery meetings with a whole new attitude, starting with gratitude rather than a judgment about the imperfections of the program. I walked right into the meeting that had been my regular meeting before, ignored the turning heads, and sat right next to one of my least favorite people. I showed an interest in her and even offered to take her to meetings. Rather than being an observer, I got involved in any way that I could.

Next, I had to get right spiritually. I was mad at God because I'd worked so hard to heal myself, and I blamed my failure on that unseen entity rather than my own will. I didn't realize how twisted my thinking was. I thought we were supposed to grow up, get married, and have a family. That seemed to be my mission in life, and when God only delivered men that I couldn't live with, it never occurred to me that I was the enemy. I deluded myself into thinking I knew what God wanted, when all along I only cared about what I wanted.

I returned to prayer, meditation, and *A Course in Miracles*, a spirituality course that teaches how to choose love over fear with a deeper commitment than just going through the motions—this time, without my own agenda, I was entitled to nothing but free will. I recognized that true freedom comes from embracing life on its terms, not by pursuing my selfish desires. Suddenly, I didn't even think about using anyone or anything. I simply walked away from addiction like any other bad relationship. It had drained me of my essence and purpose, and now I was draining the addiction of any value to me.

Instead of taking things for granted, I felt grateful for my home, family, and career—for a nice bed to sleep in, warm water, good food, nice clothes. Instead of looking for friends, I tried to be a friend, and lost friendships were restored.

I was relieved of burdensome business obligations that I'd carried for years. Even though I forgot about having a relationship, the universe sent me the perfect person. For some reason, I stopped being attracted to the bad boys and enjoyed getting to know someone without thinking of a future. My first healthy relationship evolved from a friendship into the kind of marriage I'd always longed for—a loving partnership supported by emotional availability and healthy problem-solving. I wasn't even trying, and everything was going better than I could have ever expected. The best part is that within a year, all of this happened organically, without effort or force of will on my part.

The Addiction Epidemic

Our society has a massive addiction problem, but it can be solved. It won't be solved with new laws, diets, pseudo-help, or a war on drugs. We've tried all that, and it simply hasn't worked. Hundreds of millions of people suffer from addiction, costing billions of dollars and millions of lives each year, yet the problem only grows.

Many people are unaware they're addicted. They don't see the connection between disaster and their behavior. Many people are diagnosed with mental disorders when, in reality, they have an addiction. Remove the addiction, and life becomes normal and productive. Some people think they just have a bad habit, and they waste years trying to control the behavior, all the while getting worse. Some people know they're addicted, but they don't know why they feel worse when they stop. Or maybe, like me, they've searched their whole lives and were led in many directions, and when things didn't get better, they temporarily gave up.

Setbacks are never a reason to give up. We must never relent; we need only learn and then do better. I wrote this book to help those in the addiction maze find the exit as quickly as possible, without wasting years of time and thousands of dollars.

I also write with the hope that this book will contribute to my big vision goal: that by 2030, at least one million lives will be saved and not lost to addiction. I believe one crucial step—and what I am hoping to do with this book—is to change our current perspective on addiction and publicize the best way to prevent and end addiction for good. Once people begin to accept that we have been looking at and treating addiction through primitive and ineffective models, we could reroute the billions of government and private dollars allotted to *fighting* addiction and apply those funds to *real prevention and permanent solution.* If the void never forms within us, there will be no need to fill it with toxic behavior and substances. I believe that every addiction is a substitute for love, so if we learn how to love ourselves, there will be no desire to engage in self-destructive behavior. If taken on globally, the approach offered in this book could eradicate addiction.

As you are about to find out, I believe there is only one addiction and one solution. I will explain more throughout these pages, but suffice it to say for now that until we approach addiction in this manner, millions of addicted people who want a cure will continue to suffer and fail. They will either give up one addictive behavior and find a substitute, or they will go from one form of treatment to the next without healing the underlying cause. Most likely, they will do both, but neither is an addiction solution.

The method of treatment I will offer you in the following pages both exposes the one addiction for what it is and provides the solution. Whether you're someone who is looking for a way out of addiction, you know someone with a problem, or you are a professional who wants to better serve your patients, I wrote this book for you. I can tell you from decades of personal experience and working with thousands of patients, there is a path to freedom from addiction and suffering. If you are willing to follow the guidance, you can exit the maze of addiction *forever*.

I suggest you approach the exercises in this book with a commitment and desire to heal like none other. Nothing will work without a desire to get well. Plan to move through the material gradually. It may take weeks or even months to read the material and do the exercises at the end of each chapter. I suggest you buy yourself a journal to keep your answers in one place, so you can turn to and reflect on them as you come to better understand yourself.

Give yourself the gift of taking the time needed to digest the contents and to reach a sense of calm understanding before you go on to the next section. Equally important, no matter how much you might think you know already, is reading with an open mind and heart. Many of us know a lot, but we haven't learned a thing. The information provided is based on healing techniques that do work, but only when you implement them and follow through.

If you are like most people who struggle with addiction, you probably had a vision for your life, but something interrupted that dream and pulled you into a different paradigm. Imagine right now what your life would look like if you were living your greatest dreams. The following pages can remove the barriers blocking your success, bring you back to yourself, and wake up the person you were meant to be.

If you're stuck in the maze and you want to get out, now is the time. Somewhere in the maze, there is an exit sign, and my intention is to help you find it.

PART 1

ONE ADDICTION

To overcome the addiction epidemic, the first thing we need to let go of is the idea that there are multiple addictions. I'm not referring to "cross-addiction," the treatment industry's term for switching from one addiction to another. The truth is there is only one. Until we face this fact, treatment will continue to be just another dysfunctional system. It's time to stop fooling around with people's lives and get right to the point. Addiction is addiction. We need to recognize that once someone has become addicted, simply ending an addictive behavior does not mean that the addiction is cured; it means only that the behavior has stopped.

Let's use alcoholism as an example. An alcoholic stops drinking. They faithfully attend Alcoholics Anonymous (AA) meetings, get their white poker chip (or other symbol of commitment to stop gambling with their lives and stay sober), and stay in touch with their sponsor, all great things to do. But just as often, alcoholics simultaneously take up a "new" addiction, whether it be sugar, sex, caffeine, nicotine, or something else. When this is the case, why do we say these people are "on the wagon"? Are they really "sober"? I say no; they are still under the influence of addiction, still trapped in the maze, and it's high time we start to acknowledge that they are using a substitute behavior to continue the same pattern of addiction, the same pattern of (emotional) avoidance. I assure you that for most people who struggle with addiction, this is more the norm than the exception. Eventually, all these alternative ways of self-medicating lead back to square one: another corridor in the maze.

If we continue to treat only the symptoms (addictive behaviors), no one will ever be cured. When we fail to address the force that drove a person to become an addict, we can never go beyond the behavior and find the underlying cause that continues to power the addiction train.

This might be a depressing thought to someone who imagines that giving up something represents losing a "pleasure" in their life, but I'd like you to rethink the word *pleasure*. Pleasure is a state in which you feel good. A candy bar, a cocktail, a joint, an orgasm, a new suit—all make you feel good. I want you to replace temporary high feelings with learning how to feel good about yourself most of the time. Then short-term, fake, induced feelings (always followed with remorse) will be replaced with good self-esteem that doesn't need a fix.

Once we face the reality that there is only one addiction, we get to give up the illusion that addressing only the symptoms can heal it. Then, and only then, is a real solution possible.

1

A DISEASE OF DENIAL

> I have absolutely no pleasure in the stimulants in which
> I sometimes so madly indulge. . . . It has been in the desperate
> attempt to escape from torturing memories . . . from a sense
> of insupportable loneliness and a dread of some strange
> impending doom.
>
> —Edgar Allan Poe

Substance abuse alone costs our nation more than $600 billion annually,[1] even though the public, as well as many mental health professionals, still fail to understand what addiction looks like. Abuse of tobacco, alcohol, and illicit drugs costs us more than $740 billion annually related to crime, lost work productivity, and health care.[2] Advertisers trade on the idea that if you're not happy, you just need more unhealthy food, more medication, more money, more sex, more, more, more.

Technology has taken addiction to a whole new level, especially since COVID-19.[3] Computers and cell phones have become the new baby-sitters. This results in less parental bonding and programs a child's brain for instant gratification. We expect everything to be delivered on demand. Patiently waiting for something is practically considered old fashioned behavior—if it's not on speed dial, forget it. We can speed up some things, but the world will turn at its own rate. If we can't accept this reality, we are destined to become frustrated, irrational people who are prone to self-medicate to rid ourselves of such unwanted emotions.

So many of us have become affected, but addiction has yet to be univer-sally recognized as a progressive disease. Many people have a stereotypical image of an addict as someone in the throes of extreme behavior—broke, staggering, homeless, or institutionalized. Not true. The street addict didn't start out homeless but wound up there. Most of the addicts with whom I have worked are high-functioning members of society—that is, until they discover that they can no longer "manage" their addiction when they hit an emotional bottom, lose a relationship, or fail at a lucrative career and go broke. The famous and wealthy people with whom I have worked have had to hit an emotional bottom before they became ready to change. Money provides more distractions and a higher likelihood of veering off a recovery course.

For example, Becky started therapy because she couldn't stay sober. She had two things going for and against her: beauty and wealth. She'd had a relatively stable life and was a happily married mother of four until her drinking became excessive. Things got so bad, her husband filed for divorce, and Becky went to treatment—but didn't stay sober. Her divorce landed her a large sum of money, and she started a business, which did quite well. The next ten years were riddled with relapsing and two more divorces, but her career success prevented her from facing the harmful role alcohol was playing in her life. Becky's emotional pain brought her to therapy, but she was unwilling to break her pattern. After two months, instead of learning how to live alone as a sober woman, she was back on a dating app and in love once again. Working on herself was secondary to all else, and predictably, she started drinking as soon as the relationship moved from the euphoric romance phase to the need for problem solving. Rather than facing her insecurities when conflicts arose, she resorted to alcohol to cope. The relationship ended with Becky back in treatment, where she met another man and started the cycle all over again. Unfortunately, Becky would have to go through a great deal more pain before she'd be willing to face herself. Her ability to attract men and enjoy financial success buffered her from the reality that her addiction to alcohol and romance were robbing her of a stable, peaceful life. Tragically, people who are incapable of facing the truth about addiction often end up with brain damage, become destitute, or even die because they can't endure the discomfort of change. The longer the pattern continues, the lower the rate of success.

With all the ways that money and fame can enable one to pursue multiple addictions, it can be harder to break through the denial. With wealth comes more distractions, more enablers, and it's harder to hit an emotional or financial bottom. At the same time, there's an incredible amount of pressure to keep producing and maintain an image. As long as they produce, they can't fathom an addiction problem. I believe this is why so many celebrities wind up overdosing or committing suicide. They are caught in two mazes at once. One is addiction, the other is the illusion that a person with money and fame can't have an addiction.

Denial is a failure to understand how addictive behavior is different from "normal" behavior. For example, normal drinkers actually can start and stop at will; therefore, they do not experience multiple hangovers, blackouts, loss of control, personality changes, or any of the other signs of a problem drinker. Normal drinkers are satisfied with a drink or two and often leave some of the beverage unconsumed. Since most alcoholics hang with other alcoholics, their peers may all agree about what's "normal," but people who don't have problems with alcohol don't have these symptoms. Normal drinkers are shocked when they experience any of these symptoms and either make sure they never exceed their limit again or stop drinking entirely. Budding alcoholics will try all kinds of tricks to avoid these symptoms, but the fact of the matter is that they have already fallen into the maze of trying *to control*. At that point, they're already in the maze, even though they don't know it yet. Society has become so conditioned to regular or heavy drinking that the maze has closed in on us and we don't want to think about stopping things we truly enjoy. We're afraid that if we do, something will be missing. We forget that it's the feeling of something missing that gets us started in bad habits in the first place.

> **Denial is a failure to see how addictive behavior is different from "normal" behavior.**

You might think that I'm overgeneralizing or being unrealistic. If so, I'd like to ask one simple question: If every time you ate an apple, you got sick, would you keep eating them? Of course not. Apples aren't addictive.

Addiction is not limited to drugs and alcohol. One thing all expressions of addiction have in common is that the symptoms grow worse over time. A food addict may gain only ten pounds a year, but in ten years, that's a hundred pounds. A sex addict may occasionally masturbate to ease an urge when no partner is available, but over time, winds up masturbating to the point of physical injury, such as Peyronie's disease. A gambler may start off having fun at a poker table but eventually will lose all posses-sions to the addiction.

After all, lots of people can take all kinds of remedies so that they can continue to do things that hurt them. Take ice cream for example. Why would someone take Lactaid pills just so they can eat ice cream without suffering lactose intolerance? The ice cream provides a soothing, happy, feeling because it's full of a highly addictive substance called sugar. Once this chemical hits the brain, it's as addictive as cocaine.[4] People who suffer lactose intolerance or gain an excessive amount of weight, continue to consume the ice cream regardless of the negative consequences and don't pay attention to what their bodies are telling them. The same is true of any addiction, feeling good for the moment overrides anything else.

Remember, addiction is continuing a behavior despite negative conse-quences. Why would someone choose to repeatedly engage in a behavior that causes suffering unless they were addicted? They are going for the feeling the addiction provides, and they either forget or don't care about the consequences because the mind focuses on the feeling they'll get, not the results.

No matter the form, addiction impacts everyone, and the longer the denial goes on, the worse the consequences become. One patient, upon the death of her husband, had a rude awakening when she had to face the realities of his secret life. He had been found dead of a cocaine overdose, reported by his sex partner—a paid prostitute. Upon investigation, it was discovered that he had spent all the couple's money on drugs, illicit sex, and gambling. She now had to face being hundreds of thousands of dollars in debt, a home in foreclosure, and two children whom she tried to protect from the truth about their father. It will take many years for this patient to put the shattered pieces of her life back together.

The reason addiction isn't detected before dire consequences occur is that most people are in denial about the symptoms. Short-term denial isn't always a bad thing; it can protect us from an overload of shock. But sometimes we've been shocked repeatedly over a long stretch of time, and we don't ever come out of denial. We simply become numb or develop the ability to let the shock bounce off us.

The denial of addiction is so subtle it doesn't allow the addicted person to see the truth. A person becomes so dependent on taking a substance or engaging in an activity to feel good that they lose touch with all the things that provide lasting fulfillment. Addiction literally hijacks the rational part of the brain that fosters self-preservation and inserts the thought that one can't be happy without their vice. Denial tells them they are fine when they're clearly not. If anyone tries to address the behavior, addicted people respond with anger, a cover-up for the fear of losing their pacifier.

I recently spoke with a woman who had completed treatment for alcoholism. She was not at all happy with her recovery; she missed her wine. When I explored her history further, she told me that prior to her excessive drinking, she'd had gastric bypass surgery (abdominal resecting that reduces the ability to eat even normal quantities), a drastic measure for weight loss. No longer able to consume as much food or the kinds of food she preferred, she replaced her old favorite pastime with drinking alcohol. It didn't take long for her to start drinking in the same way she'd been eating—around the clock. After treatment, she could indulge in neither, leaving her miserable. Like so many others who don't understand addiction, she didn't realize that she hadn't cured her addiction to food by having surgery. She merely ended up substituting alcohol for food.

> Addiction literally hijacks the rational part of the brain
> that fosters self-preservation and inserts the thought
> that one can't be happy without their vice.

How does this happen? Very easily. Here's an outline of a typical scenario, so you can see if any of this seems familiar to you. You try something and it provides a feeling you've been missing: comfort, excitement, being accepted, pleasure. You like that feeling, so you keep doing the thing. One day it hits you that things have gotten out of control, and you've gained too much weight, you've spent too much money, you've had one too many hangovers.

You take matters into your own hands and decide to do something about it. You muster up all of your willpower and you decide to quit. You make up your mind; you set a target date; it might get forwarded a few times, but eventually you stop. It's a little rough at first, but you like feeling back in control. You're losing weight, not missing work from too much partying; your finances improve; people aren't mad at you anymore, and you feel relieved. But after a period of time (short or long), it seems you're getting a whisper in your ear: *It's been a long time; you've regained control, so it's okay to indulge just a little. After all, you're not supposed to be perfect, and you deserve a little treat for how good you've been. Not only that, but life has been pretty boring lately, and it's time to do something enjoyable. Since you have control now, you can fudge just a little, and everything will be fine. It's only for one occasion, and you'll get right back on track.*

And then when you sink your teeth into that first piece of creamy chocolate frosted cake, or have that first glass of your favorite wine, or you feel the thrill of risky living, it's almost as good as the first time. It's so good you can't wait to do it again; the promise of doing it only one time has vanished from your mind. The cycle of on and off continues ad infinitum, until you finally give up altogether and don't even try to stop. At this point, your mind has been taken over by your addiction.

Addiction is similar to being slowly killed with rat poison; too often, by the time the symptoms appear, a person is so deep into the maze they can't get out. Alcoholics Anonymous warns that most untreated alcoholics wind up insane or dead.[5] *Merriam-Webster Dictionary* defines insanity as "extreme folly or unreasonableness."[6] Recovery meetings often warn, "Insanity is repeating the same mistakes and expecting different results."[7] The insanity of addiction can be literal due to brain damage from constant exposure to alcohol and other toxic substances resulting in loss of judgment, such as drinking while driving, starting fights, and other high risk behaviors. These acts often cause accidental death, death from poor health such as cirrhosis of the liver, and suicide. When a particular behavior continually leads to suffering, how could that be sane thinking?

The user rationalizes the symptoms to the point that health, mental soundness, or both become so severely impaired that they can no longer deny the problem exists. Unfortunately, many don't acknowledge the problem until the physical consequences (brain damage, bad health, insanity) become irreversible or the addict has lost everything of material or emotional importance.

The addict isn't the only one living in denial. There's usually a person in the addict's life who enables the addict. Enablers, often referred to as "codependents," are addicted to the addict and demonstrate all the same signs and symptoms of addiction. The enabler could be an employer, a spouse, a friend, or a family member—anyone who unconsciously benefits by protecting the addict from the consequences of their choices. The codependent person relies on the addict in some way—emotionally, financially, or otherwise. Another scenario is when there is an unconscious collusion between two addicts: "I won't interfere with your addiction if you don't bug me about mine."

To illustrate what codependency looks like, here's a recap of a conversation I witnessed between an addiction counselor and a patient who was codependent with her on-and-off boyfriend:

Girlfriend: I don't understand why you told my boyfriend that he needed to go to AA. He said if I got back with him, he'd stop drinking and drugging.

Therapist: You're the one who told me he was driving drunk and his personality had changed drastically. You also told me that when he drinks, he can't stop. When I gave him an evaluation, he had quite a few symptoms.

Girlfriend: Yes, but that was only a few occasions.

Therapist: You told me when he drinks, he loses control and his personality changes and you fight.

Girlfriend: But that's why he never drinks.

Therapist: But then he does drink again in spite of the negative consequences.

Girlfriend: I just think you're judging him; I don't agree.

Therapist: I'm not judging him. I'm recognizing signs and symptoms of an illness. Just like any illness, it's best to diagnose it early.

Girlfriend: Well, I don't agree that he has signs of alcoholism; he just screwed up a few times.

Therapist: Tell me again why you keep breaking up with him?

Girlfriend: Because he had issues, but I think it was his parents who screwed him up; they were definitely big drinkers.

Clearly, the patient's girlfriend was in denial, and her refusal to even consider that her boyfriend might have symptoms of alcoholism enabled him to continue his self-destructive patterns instead of getting help. This is not only damaging to the addict, but it's dangerous for the codependent too, as they will often experience the same, or worse, impacts as the addict. The codependent is addicted to the addict and has the same behaviors and consequences—unsuccessful attempts at controlling themselves or the addict, emotional pain, financial loss, loss of friends and family, poor health, lowered self-esteem, and the gamut of other symptoms.

The codependent is often acting based on unconscious fear. They are either afraid of losing some personal benefit if the addict changes, or they fear losing the addict altogether and ending up alone.

Here are a couple more examples.

One patient, Karen, started therapy because she was depressed. Though her life had been full of losses (including a father she loved dearly), there were reasons she wasn't healing. She was addicted to cigarettes and food, was a heavy drinker, and had no problem supplementing with benzodiazepines if she needed a "break." All of these substances were to self-medicate and contributed to her depression and inability to move forward. Karen lived with a man, Jerry, whom she took care of financially. In exchange, he took care of their large home, bought groceries, and prepared meals. He also made sure to sabotage Karen's progress by drinking her favorite wine in front of her, stirring up arguments, and refusing to get a job. Their codependency kept them locked in a lose-lose relationship.

> **The codependent is often acting based on unconscious fear.**

Another family sought therapy for their daughter, Linda, whom they had taken to numerous therapists for help. No one had evaluated Linda for substance abuse and instead treated her for mental illness. During our sessions, it became clear Linda's first problem was addiction. Linda had started smoking and using drugs when she was a teen. By the time she went to college, her drinking had accelerated to the point that she didn't attend classes and flunked out. She made up reasons why she couldn't go to class, and her parents bought into her stories. Rather than insisting she get a job, they allowed her to get an apartment off campus. A few years later, she met someone and got married. Naturally, when Linda's husband realized his wife isolated and drank all day and couldn't contribute to the marriage, he wanted out. Her dad allowed her to come back home instead of insisting Linda stand on her own two feet. By now, she's on prescription drugs including Valium, smokes pot, and has had several car accidents related to drugs. Fast-forward fifteen years, Linda has had two more divorces and no career, even though she has all the talent and intelligence to accomplish just about anything. She's had numerous physical injuries from falling while drunk. When asking her father why he didn't insist she get help and stop enabling her, he'd only shake his head and say he's afraid that something terrible will happen to her if he lets go: "she might get hurt," "she can't take care of herself," "she has mental problems." Of course, he's 100 percent correct, but only because his fear of her inadequacy has disabled her from ever maturing or facing the things that have prevented her success. At age forty-five, she's still functioning as if she were thirteen, and as time goes on, she will find it harder to figure things out. Additionally, the more Linda continues to use drugs, the more her brain will become damaged and the less likely of ever fully recovering. Her father's fear of losing his daughter was coming true, but not because he was letting go or holding her accountable, but instead because he was holding on and refusing to face the facts. As time went on, Linda became more dependent on her father, who unconsciously helped her go deeper into the maze and become less capable of reaching for the stars.

The above two examples are typical when working with the families of addicts. Since many people only see addiction when someone is staggering around, goes missing for days, goes broke, or overdoses, it's easier to deny the facts than to intervene before it's too late. As long as the enabler/codependent sees the limitations in their loved one and not the possibilities, they will all remain trapped in the addiction maze.

This is why it's vital that we (and by "we," I mean doctors, therapists, and laypeople) recognize the signs and symptoms, so we can intervene before it's too late. As I will discuss later, addiction, like any illness, has symptoms and phases. The sooner we can recognize the early signs of someone's mind being hijacked with addiction, the better the chance of an early recovery.

We don't have to wait until a person has completely lost their mind—the ability to reason, to make life-saving decisions—before we recognize that a person has an addiction illness. If not, the damage to one's self-esteem and brain is so great, that it's often too late.

2

THE DIAGNOSIS DELUSION

> For me, it is far better to grasp the Universe as it really is than to
> persist in delusion, however satisfying and reassuring.
> —Carl Sagan, *The Demon-Haunted World*

The current models for addiction diagnosis and treatment have failed to adequately help those who are addicted, and often end up thwarting a person's chances of full recovery. As you're about to see, diagnosis criteria are inconsistent from one professional body to another, and none provides a comprehensive view. This greatly reduces the chances that a person suffering with an addiction will be properly diagnosed and receive the necessary treatment so they can heal.

I wish there were one perfect diagnostic model, but there's not. Each method of diagnosis has its shortcomings, the most common being a failure to recognize that all the various addictive behaviors are symptoms of one addiction.

The American Psychiatric Association (APA) changed the term *addiction* to *substance use disorder*, which is defined as the compulsive use of substances in spite of negative consequences.[1] The APA claims the most severe cases *might* be addictions.[2] This diagnosis is limited to substances and excludes the hundreds of other compulsive behaviors that, when repeated, cause people to suffer horrific consequences. The reference to "severe cases" is problematic because the refusal to recognize the early stages of addictions thwarts early intervention.

The American Psychological Association (also APA) refers to *addiction* as a chronic brain *disorder* that is influenced by biological (genetic), environmental (trauma), and psychological (mental health) factors, resulting in neurological changes that cause cravings for a drug or activity and the inability to regulate these behaviors.[3] While there is some agreement on the brain disorder concept, we must ask, where is the evidence to support that babies are born with addictive brain disorders? Since we don't give babies alcohol, drugs, sugar, and so forth, how do we know they're born with an addictive brain? Even if there is a genetic predisposition making them more susceptible, this doesn't mean that a person has to ever start an addiction. A baby isn't born as an addiction-seeking individual. While we spend decades debating what came first, the chicken or the egg, people are dying. Regardless of the cause, once a person starts getting high (from whatever achieves that goal), the craving develops (sometimes quickly, sometimes slowly), and over time, the brain becomes disordered from ongoing abuse.

> Each method of diagnosis has its shortcomings,
> the most common being a failure to recognize that
> all the various addictive behaviors are symptoms
> of one addiction.

However, unless the brain has become too damaged, with abstinence and proper nutrition,[4] exercise and healthy lifestyle,[5] the brain is capable of reparation.[6] And since the evidence is clear that certain things are addictive because they induce cravings, why not include these specific substances and behaviors as highly addictive and likely to change your brain chemistry? This view does not explain the demise of people who regularly become addicted involuntarily, like those who sustain traumatic injuries and, while unconscious, are given highly addictive narcotics such as morphine and hydromorphone and awake to find themselves chemically dependent before they realize what has happened. The prescription opioid crisis—for pain certainly didn't start as voluntary use—has resulted in an addiction rate of 20 to 30 percent, and 50,000 recent annual deaths.[7]

The Society of Addiction Psychology (Division 50 of the American Psychological Association) has recognized multiple addictive behaviors that include a list of compulsions beyond substance abuse, such as gambling, eating, sexual behavior, and spending.[8] Again, this diagnosis is limited to the same meager list as the other organizations, even though millions of people engaging in myriad of other behaviors (caffeine, nicotine, work, video gaming, and so forth) suffer the exact same symptoms. Even though each of the above organizations defines addiction in its own way, most mental health professionals refer to the *Diagnostic and Statistical Manual of Mental Disorders (DSM)* or the *International Statistical Classification of Diseases and Related Health Problems (ICD)* as their primary guide for diagnosis and treatment recommendations. The *DSM* recognizes just two kinds of addiction, although the manual does not call it that; instead, it describes substance use (alcohol, cannabis, hallucinogens, opioids, sedatives, stimulants, and tobacco) and gambling disorders. These disorders are defined by the inability to control how much and for how long, despite psychological and physical withdrawal and preoccupation.[9] Both manuals avoid the word *addiction*, and neither one extends the diagnosis to other behaviors with the same symptoms.

In 2011, the American Society of Addiction Medicine (ASAM) redefined addiction as "a treatable, chronic medical disease involving complex interactions among brain circuits, genetics, the environment, and an individual's life experiences. People with addiction use substances or engage in behaviors that become compulsive and often continue despite negative consequences."[10] This is the best definition thus far. ASAM also points out that several factors can trigger the addictive response. Even if the drug of choice is not within reach, any stimulus associated with using it (an ad, a memory, a smell, and so forth) can trigger the craving.[11] This phenomenon was demonstrated by the researcher Ivan Pavlov, who rang a bell every time he fed a group of dogs. After a few trials, the dogs salivated every time they heard a bell ring, regardless of whether or not food was present. ASAM took a big step for mankind by recognizing "other behaviors," but they haven't yet taken the giant leap that it's all one addiction.

Alcoholics Anonymous (AA) provides a self-diagnostic questionnaire that pinpoints symptoms: failed attempts at stopping or limiting amounts of consumption, switching from one type of alcohol to another, morning drinking, problems related to drinking, missed work, and blackouts.[12] The symptoms listed are congruent with the aforementioned criteria, but someone who has an alcohol problem and doesn't understand addiction as a progressive illness might look at these questions and say, "So what? Doesn't everyone have these symptoms every once in a while?"

Actually, no.

The new normal might be greater acceptance of these symptoms, but normal drinkers enjoy a couple of drinks and that's it, they're not constantly crossing an invisible line driven by an invisible hole.

AA has helped millions of people, but it doesn't address all forms of addiction. If a member has another addiction, they are encouraged to go to a recovery meeting that specializes in that addiction. I personally spent twenty years going from one type of addiction meeting to the next. Conclusion: there should be one meeting—"Addictions Anonymous."

> It's much easier to get out of a maze if you exit early on.

Although not used as often as the above sources, there are better evaluation techniques for diagnosing addiction. My favorite is a chart that evolved from E. M. Jellinek's 1960 book, *The Disease Concept of Alcoholism*, which outlines the symptoms and phases of alcoholism.[13] He developed an inverted bell-shaped curve that outlines the progressive symptoms and phases into (and recovery from) alcoholism.[14] I find the chart applicable to any addiction. Jellinek refers to the "early-stage alcoholic," who uses alcohol to feel better, relieve anxiety, and escape emotional pain, and who, over time, experiences memory loss, keeps a stash, and increases dependency, with ever-increasing consequences.[15] The "middle-stage" symptoms are reproof by family and friends, failed attempts to control usage, violation of one's own moral standards, missed work, blackouts and health problems, and increased tolerance for the substance.[16] The "chronic-stage" includes an obsession with alcohol, withdrawal, delirium, tremors, alcohol psychosis, impaired thinking, and failed health. I like to use this chart because it identifies the early signs and symptoms before the addiction has become all-consuming and the person's life rotates around the addiction.[17] Like any illness, the sooner the diagnosis, the better the prognosis. When using this chart, I often visualize the mouse in the maze, moving from one corridor to the next, becoming more lost as it wanders and loses its ability to find its way out—it's much easier to get out of a maze if you exit early on.

The Jellinek chart also shows the progression out of the addiction and into recovery—from the desire for help and stopping the behavior to

finding a support system, self-care, therapy, and other life-saving acts.[18]
I feel the Jellinek chart is the best diagnostic technique because it provides
a comprehensive map that can be used to guide the patient and the diagnostician to track the progressive symptoms of addiction and the recovery
process in an accurate and specific manner that is applicable to all forms of
addiction. However, it does not address cross-addiction or the underlying
cause, and it should be seen as a useful process in early-stage recovery and
be followed with an emphasis on addressing the wounds that precipitated
the addiction in the first place.

When we put all of these diagnostic criteria together, we get a mish-
mash of similarities and differences. The scope of what constitutes an
addiction varies greatly. While there is some consensus on signs and
symptoms, some won't even use the word *addiction*. Nor is there agreement that the symptoms cited would apply to *any* addiction, or the fact
that all addictions are the same, and if a person has one and gives it
up, they are likely to substitute something else until the root cause is
addressed.

You can imagine how confusing these different interpretations are
to professionals, not to mention laypeople. Picture a person going from
professional to professional and getting totally different interpretations of
their problem. "We don't call your problem an addiction; you have a brain
disorder." "You have a gambling addiction, but not alcohol addiction—
that's a substance use disorder." "The reason you can't quit smoking is
because you have a brain disease." Of course, the brain gets dysregulated
from constant overstimulation and abuse. But why not eliminate possible
causes that might be other than organic. How is the public supposed to
be helped with so much contradiction among the professionals? Pretty
crazy, huh?

Where All Diagnoses Miss the Mark

Most problematic is that in every case, the addictive behavior is seen as
the problem rather than the symptom of an underlying cause. This is at
the crux of why so many people fail to get diagnosed and why, even when
the diagnosis is accurate and a particular compulsive behavior stops, the
addiction rarely ends. Treatments that are considered "successful" often

mean that the patient has simply switched from one addictive behavior to another.

During the thirty years I've spent in my practice as of this writing, I've seen multiple examples of misdiagnosis and the subsequent consequences. Three classic ones that I see most frequently are mistaking grief and trauma for a mood disorder, such as anxiety or depression; misperceiving an existing addiction as a mood disorder; and prescribing narcotics to someone who is in recovery and failing to recognize the probability of relapse into another form. The following cases describe each of these three common errors clinicians make.

> **The addict hears what the addict wants to hear:**
> **Drugs are good for you.**

One example of mistaking addiction as a mood disorder occurred with a patient of mine whom I'll call Mary. As a child she had been sexually and verbally abused by her father. She was prescribed an antidepressant and Valium for anxiety. Her physician never asked her why she was anxious or explored the source of her depression, but he did make sure to tell her, "This is a chemical imbalance in your body, and you will always need medication." When a physician so authoritatively makes such a declaration, it tends to become a fixed thought in a person's mind—especially an addict's mind. The addict hears what the addict wants to hear: Drugs are good for you.

It's bad enough that this patient was abused as a child, but it was even worse that a doctor told her she could wipe away all the pain of that abuse with a pill. The message here is: *It's not okay to be upset with the fact that your own parent violated your trust, took advantage of you, and left a wound on you that you would carry for the rest of your life.* I'm not sure which form of abuse is worse: to be harmed as a child or for a professional to disavow the emotional pain that needs to be purged. Medicating the pain may only drive it even deeper into the unconscious, where it may never escape.

Over the next twenty years, Mary cycled between alcohol and Valium with an ever-increasing dependence on both. She was scared to stop taking the medication because she'd been told that medication was the only treatment for her condition. Exploring the root cause, as we did, had never been presented to her as an alternative. She had spent most of her life numbed out on substances, yet she had grown tired of being medicated, so she sought therapy and mustered up the courage to investigate why she couldn't get better and discover her real self.

Mary's case presents an example of mistaking an unresolved trauma for a mood disorder, which led to addiction. Mary had gone to a psychiatrist for depression because she was sad most of the time. She didn't have the energy to do anything, and her interest in family and friends had diminished to almost nothing. She told the psychiatrist she'd been in treatment years before for cocaine, but no one had told her to stay away from all mood-altering substances. No one warned her that her brain wouldn't know the difference. No one asked or realized that, even though she had stopped using illicit drugs, she continued to drink alcohol and take Valium.

The psychiatrist had prescribed an antidepressant, but when Mary didn't improve, she was referred to a psychotherapist, and after years of counseling, she remained depressed. All the while she'd been drinking alcohol every night in increasing amounts, which made it impossible for her antidepressant to work. When Mary was referred to me, she was shocked to hear my suggestion that if she were not saturating her brain with a depressive drug every night, she might be able to benefit from therapy. She had never been shown the connection between her persistent sense of depression and the fact that she was consuming large amounts of alcohol and Valium (both of which are depressive drugs) every day. Valium is supposed to be used for several months and then stopped, but I've yet to hear of a patient whose doctor stopped prescribing it after a few months. Also, the typical warning is to avoid alcohol, but what does that mean? Why not just say "Don't drink?" Mary's doctor asked her if she drank, and Mary said occasionally, a typical response for a problem drinker. He did not tell her to abstain entirely. Alcohol was fueling her depression and when the alcohol wore off, her anxiety intensified along with her need for Valium—a vicious cycle. Once she stopped both, (under her physician's instructions) she was able to go deeper in her therapy and heal the core of her pain and suffering. A year into therapy, Mary was off all medication.

Brian, who was in recovery, was prescribed narcotics, exemplifying the second common misstep by therapists. Brian went to a psychiatrist because he was suffering from anxiety. He'd been sober for a year, and he couldn't sleep. His mind was spinning. A physical exam provided him with a clean bill of health. The psychiatrist told him he was suffering from anxiety and prescribed Valium, which produces the same relaxed feelings as having a drink, and Ambien for sleep, another mood-altering drug that is unsafe for recovering addicts. Brian found himself taking the Valium every couple of hours during the night because he liked the effect of feeling high. When his anxiety did not subside, his psychiatrist told him he needed psychotherapy. His new therapist, not an addiction counselor, failed to see that Brian was in relapse. Brian liked having someone to talk to, so he continued therapy even though he wasn't getting better. The only thing he accomplished was relapsing and adding three new rewards (Valium, Ambien, and therapy) to keep him running in his maze.

Before prescribing pills, doctors could teach patients how to master anxiety. The physical reactions in the body that signal danger result from fear-based thoughts. Something triggers a scary thought, and the body responds by releasing chemicals designed to strengthen a person's response to real danger. Most of these thoughts have no basis, but if we focus on them, the body will respond accordingly. But you can change the channel anytime and replace a fear-based thought with a peaceful one while remembering to breathe.

In Brian's case, after detoxing under a doctor's care, we worked on how to control his anxiety. He learned how to close his eyes, take several deep breaths, and be aware of the thoughts that were fueling his fears—*Someone is trying to hurt me. I'm all alone.* He then continued to breathe, even if he felt he couldn't, and replaced the fear-based thought with, *I'm safe right now.* As he continued to practice breathing through the fears and calming himself down, he successfully mastered the technique, and it didn't take long for him to realize he never needed mood-altering pills to cope with life. This in conjunction with intensive psychotherapy to heal the underlying emotional trauma allowed Brian to remain abstinent from all mood-altering substances and regain his sober-support system.

To illustrate the third example, take Raymond. On the verge of relapsing with drugs and alcohol, Raymond decided he needed help. He'd already been to therapy because, after two years of sobriety, he felt worse than when he was drinking. He'd spent his whole life using a bottle to nurse his emotional wounds, and now that he'd put it down, he could barely tolerate his emotional ups and downs. Recovery meetings weren't enough. He understood that he could no longer use any type of mood-altering drug, but ever since he'd gotten sober, he started eating excessive amounts of chocolate to "soothe" himself, especially at night, which had been his favorite time to drink and do drugs. Around the same time, Raymond developed an obsession with another AA member he had started dating. When he wasn't seeing his lover, his thoughts would fixate on her. He'd wonder what she was doing and who she was with, obsessing about her as if she were a drug, going through withdrawal (anxiety and sleepless nights) when he could not see her, becoming angry and agitated when he couldn't have sex on demand with her and missing work to be with her.

While it might seem that Raymond had "overcome" his addiction to drugs and alcohol, his new fixations showed that he had merely transferred his addiction from drugs and alcohol to chocolate, romance, and sex—all of which can produce the same high. A layperson might think this isn't such a bad trade-off, but Raymond was left with nagging cravings that made him feel like a caged, starving lion looking for his next meal. He was not feeling grateful for his sobriety; he still wanted to drink, and at least with alcohol and drugs, he was able to keep himself comfortably numb.

Raymond was still in the maze. He had not recovered from addiction. He merely switched to a new brand of cheese. He did not realize it was all the same addiction, and he would have to heal the underlying cause or continue to be driven by his yearnings.

All these examples are real-life situations. I've witnessed situations similar to Raymond's many times, including in my own life. Starting at age fifteen, I'd gone to numerous psychologists, all of whom failed to diagnose my addiction or see how addiction had destroyed my childhood and two marriages. Later, when I began my career as a mental health counselor, I realized the inadequacies of my professional training. Even though I'd interned in two mental health facilities, by the time I'd received my master's degree in psychology and worked in private practice, I'd had little training in mental illness or addictions. The first internship in a geriatric facility was simply talking to patients and using active listening skills.

The second at a family counseling clinic taught us behavior modification techniques and very little about what caused families to be dysfunctional in the first place. Yet when I asked patients about habits with which they were concerned, I realized almost everyone I was treating either had been raised in a family with addiction, they had an addiction themselves, or they were involved with an addicted person. Lacking the right skills to diagnose and treat these individuals, I took a proactive stance and read about and attended classes on addiction, went to recovery meetings, and consulted with treatment centers.

Having personally gone to five therapists over a ten-year period, none of whom had recognized addiction in my family or in me, I came to see that there was a competency gap among mental health providers in my community. As a result, when I did my doctoral dissertation, I developed a training program on chemical dependency for nurses and mental health professionals at Palm Beach Community College (now Palm Beach State College) in Lake Worth, Florida, so they could get continuing education credits, learn about the signs and symptoms of addiction, and make appropriate referrals.

When I started to quantify the need for this type of community education, I set out to measure their level of knowledge about the signs and symptoms of alcoholism. The quiz had twenty questions, all of which asked about the signs and symptoms of alcoholism. The results were shocking. Only one person scored above 70 percent.

Through a collaborative effort between the college's continuing education director, Robert Bozzone, executive director at Comprehensive Alcohol and Rehabilitation Program (CARP), and myself, we implemented the training program in 1990. As of this writing, that program has evolved into a comprehensive addiction studies program offering college credit and meeting the requirements for the Florida Certification Board for addiction.[19]

Currently, there's plentiful education on addiction, and in spite of the inconsistent criteria for diagnosis, it would behoove every mental health professional to be certified in this area of expertise. Additionally, I would recommend a self-diagnosis with the Jellinek chart (easily found on the internet), or the Five-Minute Self-Evaluation: Addiction Questionnaire located in the appendix of this book.

Redefining Addiction

Proper diagnosis is the key to the cure. People can't get well if their condition is not correctly defined. An addicted person cannot recover if the very people treating them do not understand the problem. Just like it would be intolerable if doctors consistently diagnosed cancer as heart disease, we need to start calling out addiction for what it is—persistent and deadly. A person can become addicted to anything: alcohol, drugs, exercise, food, gambling, another person, nicotine, vaping, prescription narcotics, religion, shopping, self-help programs, sex, power, video games, work, and the list goes on. Addicts are all searching for the same thing—a moment of euphoria. Whether it's the cigarette smoker with lung cancer who keeps smoking, the workaholic with chronic chest pains on the verge of a massive coronary, or the guy who's headed for divorce because his wife keeps walking in on him while he's on a porn site, they all share the same symptoms.

> **Proper diagnosis is the key to the cure.**

Addiction temptations are everywhere. I recently received a call from a brokenhearted woman because she was losing her husband to another thing. Yes, a thing called porn. She said they'd had a good relationship until suddenly he started acting strange. She thought maybe he was having an affair, but then she understood why his behavior changed, when she walked in on him while he was on a porn site. They got help, but he could not stop. I could feel her pain down to the tips of my toes when she told me she didn't know what happened to her kind, sweet, loving husband, who now had turned into a complete stranger.

Here's another example: Jeremy's marriage was crumbling because of his workaholism. He'd put in twelve to fifteen hours a day, and by the time he got home, he'd be so wound-up he'd belt down a couple of double scotches to just unwind. He'd pass out on the couch and then get up at six o'clock and start all over again. His wife appreciated the lifestyle Jeremy provided, but the kids felt fatherless, and she felt like a single mom.

Jeremy had become so addicted to work that he had no time for his family, who needed his attention. He was missing out on precious memories—something he could never get back.

Even worse, rather than science helping people get free of addiction, science is helping people find new and better ways to stay addicted. For example, e-cigarettes keep the smoker hooked on nicotine without the additives and tars of tobacco. Naltrexone allows alcoholics and addicts to keep using without getting the same high. Pills allow people to keep temporarily calm without discovering the source of their anxiety. All of these solutions deliver the message *stay addicted*. Rather than helping addicts get out of the maze, the medical world has joined them. Each of the examples in these chapters put the person in the position of behaving like a mouse in a maze looking for cheese.

The current death rate from addictive behaviors (mostly alcohol, drugs, food, and smoking) is staggering. According to the World Health Organization, over three million die annually from alcohol abuse,[20] 130 people a day (47,450 annually) die from opioid overdose (during the COVID-19 pandemic that number hit 75,361),[21] and obesity occurs in nearly half of all adults and 20 percent of children in the U.S. and is the cause of four million deaths worldwide.[22] Globally, tobacco is the cause of seven million deaths per year.[23] In 2019, there were more than fourteen thousand deaths from heroin.[24] In 2021, 100,306 drug overdose deaths were reported, according to the Centers for Disease Control and Prevention.[25] Many overdose deaths are due to fentanyl, a highly lethal, synthetic opiate added to other drugs to intensify their effect.[26] Every fifteen minutes, a baby is born suffering from opioid withdrawal.[27] This is crazy! Continuing to misrepresent these deadly conditions as "disorders" is not only irresponsible, but it fails to induce clear and early intervention.

> **Rather than helping addicts get out of the maze, the medical world has joined them.**

To summarize, we need to better educate ourselves to what addiction really is and stop candy-coating it in terms that minimize its stronghold. To call it a disorder sounds like all you need to do is get things in order.

This implies that if we reregulate the brain (with medication) everything will be fine. While the brain is certainly altered by the continuous use of substances (and chemical changes from other addictions), medicating the symptoms never addresses the real problem. Someone addicted can't stop doing something that is causing great harm to themselves and others.

What's it going to take for us to wake up?

Clearly, addiction does not operate in the fashion that the medical and psychological communities have defined. I invite you to consider a better definition: *Addiction is anything a person keeps doing regardless of adverse or painful consequences.*

This definition might seem oversimplified, but no rational, non-addicted person continues to do anything at the expense of personal health or financial security, or risks the loss of family and friends. An addicted person has lost the ability to see clearly and to stop *and stay stopped*. Examples include the alcoholic who keeps drinking in spite of numerous DUIs and illnesses; the gambler who gets into debt then borrows and steals to cover bets; the drug addict who keeps increasing the dose until they overdose; the opioid addict who remains on massive amounts of pain medication years after an injury; the food addict who is now obese, diabetic, and on the verge of a massive heart attack, yet continues to eat in a way that exacerbates their illness. These are only a few examples of people who may think they are in control, but really they are addicts in the maze.

They may even *temporarily* stop, but it doesn't take long for thoughts, such as *I can have just a little; this time it will be different*, to draw the addict deeper into the maze. Because as long as the addict is using willpower to stay away from the addiction, the battle will become so exhausting that eventually they are bound to give in to their compulsive thoughts. Addiction is sometimes like the sound of a pounding drum and relapsing seems like the only way to stop the noise—but the noise doesn't mean anything, and you can tune it out.

By the time Sherry came to see me, she'd lost everything—her home, her kids, her looks, her dignity and self-respect. She'd started as an occasional drinker: a couple of drinks socially, then every weekend, and then every night, with her starting time moving up earlier and earlier. The more she drank, the more she needed to drink to escape the consequences of her drinking. Even after she'd been arrested for driving under the influence, she'd stay in bed in the morning, neglecting to properly care for her two children and unable to hold down a job. She swore off drinking many times but always found herself in a bar with friends as she journeyed further into the maze.

Her husband said he would file for divorce and take custody of the kids if Sherry came home drunk again. She went to see a therapist who put her on an antidepressant, and she was able to stay sober for a couple of weeks, but one night while out to dinner with a friend, she forgot her husband's warning and ordered a glass of wine. For the umpteenth time, like so many people who suffer alcoholism, she told herself that since she'd been sober for a couple of weeks, she could handle having one drink. Within minutes, once the alcohol hit her brain, she forgot all about the pain and suffering alcohol had brought her. She drove home and staggered up her walkway at three o'clock in the morning. When she tried to get in the house, all the locks had been changed, and she had to sleep in her car.

When she awoke, her family was gone, and she had to stay with a relative. Three months later, she was divorced with no money, no family, no career, no life, and still she continued to drink. In spite of losing everything dear to her, she had deluded herself into thinking that her spouse and kids left because they didn't love her, even though her now ex-husband had told her he would still help her if she sobered up. She continued to try to control her drinking and continued to fail. She could not accept the fact that she was powerless to moderate her drinking and that whenever she had that first drink, she was unable to predict what would happen, how much she would consume, where she would wake up, or what she would say or do—even though alcohol had cost her everything near and dear to her!

Sherry's former husband attended her second therapy session and pleaded with her to get sober. He told her their children needed her, and he needed her too. She broke into tears and said she couldn't. My heart broke for this family. Sherry was so far along in the addiction, it seemed there was too much brain damage and she'd lost her ability to reason. Sherry never returned to therapy, though her husband came in for a few sessions in an attempt to understand her actions and to grieve.

Other than the preferred reward, the alcoholic who continues to drink is no different than the excitement junkie who continues to shoplift items they can afford, despite the public shame and humiliation of being caught, or the sex addict who is arrested for soliciting prostitutes and goes for another prostitute the next week, or the food addict who binges to the point of having to purge. Other eating disorders include addiction to sugar and fats that cause obesity or the other extremes, calorie counting to maintain an unhealthy low weight (anorexia).

Though it may take years, once a person develops the habit of denial and repetition compulsion, they succumb to the mental obsession. Just the thought of getting the fix triggers the dopamine receptors in the brain and the chase is on. Just as Pavlov described with his salivating dogs and the sound of the bell, anything that activates the mental image sets the addiction wheels into motion. It is like falling into a deep hole without a rope; when you try to get out, you make a little progress as you dig your fingers and toes into the side of the dirt wall, only to slide back down every time. Others can see the person spinning more and more out of control, but the person who is addicted is too far into the maze to see reality—or even want to.

One study by James Olds and Peter Milner demonstrates the power of the pleasure center in the brain. Rats' brains were implanted with electrodes in the septal area just above the hypothalamus, the brain's reward center.[28] In the study, the electrodes stimulated the hypothalamus every time the rat pushed a lever. The rats compulsively pushed the lever, up to two thousand times per hour, to the point that they would refuse to eat, avoid sex, abandon their young, run across electrical shock grids, or do anything to get another hit. The researchers finally had to end the experiment before the rats died of starvation.[29] People who are addicted exhibit the same type of behavior; they will push the limits to the extreme, risking everything they value to get the reward, even if it means losing it all, including their own lives.

This leads me to the biggest problem of all: even when a person gives up one addictive pattern, they usually find another to take its place. I have yet to work with someone in recovery who didn't (unknowingly) transfer their addiction another form (i.e., the addict who stops drugging and starts drinking, the recovering smoker who switches to sugar, the recovering alcoholic who tries to fill the hole with love or sex addiction)—a bottomless pit, never able to be filled.

All addicted people follow the same diagnostic criteria of being powerless to control their addiction—permanently. Like any illness, it can be cured, but it can't reverse itself. Once the person has become addicted, there is no reversing the control factor. An alcoholic will never learn how to drink alcohol moderately. A gambler will never bet controlled amounts. A food addict will never control the intake of foods to which they are addicted. While it is normal for most addicts to relapse, the focus must be on recovery and healing. Only with abstinence can a person get enough distance from the behavior to begin to understand that any manifestation of addiction must be replaced with genuine self-love, or the drive to use another way will remain.

> **Even when a person gives up one addictive pattern,
> they usually find another to take its place.**

If all this sounds discouraging, take heart. By the time you finish reading this book, you may see your addiction as a blessing in disguise. You may come to realize that addiction has a purpose. It presents an opportunity to heal something much deeper, and if you do the work, it can lead you on a path to genuine self-love.

Pretty soon, I'm going to show you how you can find your way out of the maze and be free of addiction once and for all. But first, I'm going to share with you how we need to rethink treatment, so not only can you see that there is a solution, but you'll also get a good sense of how you can achieve it. I'm going to give you a map out of the maze.

Self-Evaluation Questionnaire

Identify Things You've Tried to Control

1. Have you ever felt that you have tried to control something but were unsuccessful? Describe those situations.
2. When you were unsuccessful, describe what happened.
3. Have you ever been in counseling to try to control a particular behavior? If so, what?

4. Were you successful? Why or why not?
5. If you have tried to stop doing something multiple times, have you given up on trying?
6. Write down a time in your life when you felt stuck at something.
7. Describe someone you know who has an addiction. If you knew the person before they became addicted, did you see warning signs? If so, describe them.
8. What do you think that person's life would be like if they weren't addicted?

3

THE TREATMENT TRAP

I have not failed ten thousand times. I've successfully found ten
thousand ways that will not work.
—Thomas Edison

The current models for treating addiction rely on strategies that are
as effective as trying to teach a mouse to stop pushing the lever that
dispenses the morphine. The reason is that the most utilized treatment
strategies focus on stopping the addiction (the symptom), not healing the
cause—which is a void in the person. And to remedy that, we must fill
that void with self-love—meaning and purpose.

Abstinence will stop the behavior, but it doesn't change the void that
continues to look for something to fill it. All willful attempts to stop or
reduce the addictive behavior only intensify the obsession. Studies have
shown that for heavy drinkers, parts of the brain that can help control a
drinking habit are damaged, which makes the pursuit of moderation not
just a matter of will but a physical impossibility.[1]

Any reference I make to treatment for substances applies to all flavors of addiction because they are all expressions of the same disease.
The treatment models are pretty much the same also—you give up the
thing to which you are addicted. There are exceptions. Obviously, for
food, you would abstain from the foods you are addicted to—usually
wheat and sugar—and learn to eat healthily. For sex, you would abstain
from harmful sexual behaviors and replace those with healthy sexual intimacy. Note that even though not all compulsive behaviors have to be
medically detoxed, all do have components of emotional and physical
withdrawal—the jonesing effect that shows up across any manifestation
of addiction—and are always painful.

> Abstinence will stop the behavior, but it doesn't
> change the void that continues to look for
> something to fill it.

For example, Rex describes his withdrawal symptoms from sex and love addiction. "I can't stop this pattern with my girlfriend, or ex-girlfriend, whatever she is. Eight years ago, we met in a bar and hit it off. I went home with her that night, and the sex was superhot. We wound up seeing each other every day. Then she saw a text on my phone from someone else, and the trouble started. We've been on and off for the past five years. We break up, and I feel relieved for a day or two, and I distract myself by hooking up with someone on an app. But after a few days, I start thinking about how good sex is with my ex. I find myself obsessing about calling her, and I get angry with myself, call myself a stupid idiot, but after a week, I'm depressed; I can't sleep; I can't eat. Somehow, we always manage to run into one another, and I literally shake inside like a surge of adrenaline. Within a day or two we're back in the sheets for the most incredible sex I've ever experienced. This is messed up, but I can't stop."

Rex was experiencing numerous symptoms of drug withdrawal: feeling sick, insomnia, loss of appetite, poor concentration, difficulty thinking clearly, depression.

Even though withdrawal symptoms are similar for various flavors of addiction, not all forms of withdrawal require medication. In the case of substances, it is a necessity for a medical doctor to determine the appropriate protocol.

Medication

The medical community has three ways they use medications to treat addictions: detox, psychiatric medications, and harm reduction. Detox is often medically necessary to reduce withdrawal and seizures, which in some cases can be deadly. Psychiatric medications are often used to temporarily stabilize someone who is highly anxious or depressed, and some medications are permanent.

Detox

All detox drugs are prescribed on a temporary basis to help the addict wean off the drug to which they are addicted. Hospitals, mental health facilities, and detox centers are available for detoxification from excessive amounts of alcohol or drugs. "Getting clean" is the first step of the recovery process, though not every patient intends to stop using; some just want to "dry out." Detox typically occurs in a confined setting; however, some outpatient clinics will detox patients if they have a proper caregiver at home to administer meds and watch the patient carefully. One of the disadvantages of this approach is that the recovering person does not connect with other people in treatment and remains isolated. If someone is detoxed at home, treatment should include psychotherapy and recovery meetings. Since addiction is a disease of isolation and loneliness, it's critical to find a strong support system.

There are several medications currently prescribed for specific types of detoxification.

Alcohol

Benzodiazepines (sedatives) and anticonvulsants are administered to reduce withdrawal symptoms from alcohol and the chance of seizures. Benzodiazepines can cause severe depression, psychosis, and suicidal ideology and can be deadly when mixed with alcohol.[2] Naltrexone blocks the euphoric effect of alcohol and opiates and reduces cravings during withdrawal.

Opioids

Methadone (brand names Dolophine and Methadose), buprenorphine (Suboxone, Subutex), and naltrexone (Vivitrol) are used to treat withdrawal from opioids. Most people stay on methadone indefinitely. Suboxone is supposed to be administered for several months in conjunction with psychotherapy. Suboxone, like methadone, can cause permanent dependency.[3] Naltrexone is also used to reduce alcohol and opioid cravings, some people use it to attempt normal drinking. Since it blocks the euphoric effect, if someone who uses alcohol and drugs with Naltrexone and decides they want to get high, they are more likely to overuse or even overdose when on naltrexone.[4] In other words, if your intention is to get high, these drugs won't stop you, but using while on them risks unwanted consequences.

Stimulants
Vistaril is an antihistamine that relieves itchiness, nausea, and vomiting. Norpramin is an antidepressant used to facilitate abstinence. Baclofen diminishes the effect of positive sensations associated with cocaine.

> **Since addiction is a disease of isolation and loneliness, it's critical to find a strong support system.**

Tobacco
Zyban and Chantix are supposed to be used in conjunction with group therapy to reduce craving and practice alternative behavior to prevent relapse. Nicotine replacement via patches, gum, lozenges, and sprays allows the person to remain addicted without the consequence of lung damage.

One problem with detox is that many programs do not provide the therapy necessary for long-term remission. Many patients use detox centers to medically withdraw, then start drinking or drugging again. A physician at a local hospital recently referred a patient to me who had detoxed five times within a few months. When I met with the patient, it was clear she had no intention of doing the work necessary to stay sober, especially since she was able to use the hospital as her legal drug dealer. When she couldn't stop drinking, the patient would detox on massive doses of benzodiazepines, then go on to stay sober for a week or two and repeat the pattern all over again. She simply used the detox medication to get high while she wasn't drinking.

There's no doubt some people may need long-term medication, especially in the case of dual diagnosis (an addiction combined with severe depression, bipolar disorder, or schizophrenia). Newly sober people often exhibit signs of mental illness; however, with time and a healthy lifestyle, the brain can recover and the symptoms diminish.[5]

I believe that detox centers could expand to address all manifestations of addiction. Since withdrawal from any addictive behavior has the same symptoms of anger, irritability, depression, and craving, a one- or two-week stay in a facility could ease the withdrawal. Temporary emotional support, safety, and self-care could stabilize a person, reduce chances of relapse, and prepare the person for intensive outpatient therapy and adequate support upon discharge—something that is currently lacking.

Prevention

Antabuse is a medication that is given to alcoholics after they are detoxed to prevent relapse. The patient is responsible for taking a pill that when mixed with alcohol causes nausea, dizziness, chest pain, and other unpleasant effects. It only works if taken daily, and once alcoholics decide to drink, they set the pill aside.

Psychiatric Medications

When I went to treatment in 1986, medication was rarely used. The gold standard was to wait before taking medication, go to meetings, get a sponsor, and if necessary, see a therapist. Currently, it is standard to prescribe medication during and after treatment. The push for medication is based on the disease model, strongly endorsed by the treatment industry and pharmaceutical companies, even though for decades people stayed sober without residential treatment or medication.[6]

Some medications are necessary if a person has a secondary mood or mental disorder, such as major-depressive disorder, a personality disorder, or a psychotic disorder. On the other hand, someone in emotional or physical withdrawal might exhibit all of the symptoms of mental illness, but given some time for the brain to regulate, these symptoms often subside. It is my opinion that in the past twenty years, the trend has been to prematurely render a dual diagnosis because many insurance companies will provide additional benefits for mental disorders. This is the result of multiple treatments for the same addiction, and insurance companies clamping down on payment for the same treatment repeatedly. If a patient has a mental disorder, the insurance will pay for treatment for that condition. It all boils down to money rather than the patient's well-being.

Antidepressants

In the 1980s and early 1990s, unless a patient was severely impaired, it was customary to wait a year of sobriety before prescribing antidepressant medication to people in recovery. At that time, depression had two categories. Reactive depression was due to an environmental stress, such as loss of a loved one, and was typically treated with therapy. The other type was a neurochemical imbalance, which was treated with medication. If environmentally induced stress was severe, such as the unexpected loss of a spouse or a child or being the victim of a violent crime, short-term medication was sometimes prescribed to stabilize the patient enough for them to benefit from therapy.

In 1980, when the third revision of the *Diagnostic and Statistical Manual* was released, there was an attempt to "re-medicalize" American psychiatry.[7] The *DSM-III* elected to put all depressive and manic conditions under the category of "mood disorders," and this kicked off a slow shift toward prescribing more medication for these types of diagnoses.[8] Now under the classification of mood disorders, depression due to environmental stress is regularly treated with medication, and in many cases, it is prescribed as an alternative to therapy. It has been of grave concern that the thousands of patients I've seen over the past couple of decades have been prescribed psychiatric medication (for normal sorrow and grief) and that the treatment industry has trended more and more in this direction. At the very least, a person should be given the opportunity to grieve a loss or process trauma before medicating the pain with an antidepressant.

These patients are prescribed serotonin reuptake inhibitors (SSRIs), which reduce symptoms by increasing serotonin levels in the brain. The most common drugs are Celexa, Lexapro, Paxil, Prozac, and Zoloft. These medications are not mood altering, but many who remain on them for a long period of time go through a different kind of hell wrought with the symptoms of withdrawal experienced by any addict when they stop.

One patient, Jill, struggled with an eating disorder and depression and had been on antidepressant medication for ten years. At the time, she was not happy in her marriage; her husband traveled, and she often was left alone at home with their two children. When her husband was home, he showed little interest in her, and she used food to soothe herself. Her medical doctor said she was suffering from clinical depression and prescribed an antidepressant. (Jill should have been referred to a psychotherapist first.) Two of the side effects of the medication were weight gain and decreased sexual interest, including the inability to have orgasms. During her therapy, we discussed getting to the bottom of her pain, so she could heal the feelings underlying her depression. She felt that the medication had made her emotionally numb, and she wanted to go off it, so she could "get herself back." Under her physician's care, she was weaned off the medication over a six-month period, during which Jill suffered bouts of severe anxiety, clamminess, insomnia, nightmares, obsessive thoughts, and morbid feelings in the morning, all symptoms she'd never experienced before taking antidepressants. It took over a year for Jill to begin to feel back to her old self, and she often said had she known about the side effects, she never would have started the medication.

Antianxiety Medications

Anxiety can be treated with some of the same SSRIs as depression, but sometimes anxiety is treated with a benzodiazepine, such as Valium, Xanax, or Ativan, all mood-altering substances. Like other sedative drugs, they create a sense of calm or euphoria, and for someone prone to addiction, they aren't much different than drinking or drugging away the anxiety. Again, the anxiety should be treated with psychotherapy prior to medication whenever possible.

Antipsychotic Drugs

Dopamine receptor antagonists and serotonin-dopamine antagonists are used to counteract hallucinations, severe depression, acute mania, and delusional thinking.[9] While it is critical that someone who genuinely suffers from a dual diagnosis be provided the necessary medication, I do feel a diagnosis like this should not be made in haste. A psychiatrist can order blood work to determine a true chemical imbalance, and if warranted, this should be done at regular intervals to adjust the medication as necessary. Most antipsychotic drugs are not addictive.

A person who genuinely suffers a dual diagnosis (an addiction paired with a mental disorder) will need to be on medication to stabilize their mental disorder before they can benefit from addiction treatment. Secondary disorders are treated with medicine that is not mood altering but will regulate the chemical imbalance in the brain. Someone who has a mental disorder will need to be informed that it is critical they stay on the medication.

Medication has an important place in treating addiction and mental illness. It is miraculous that a person suffering from schizophrenia, bipolar disorder, or suicidal ideation can be given a non-mood-altering pill and be asymptomatic. Further, there is little chance of these people staying sober when they are suffering from psychosis (visual and auditory hallucinations, delusional thinking) without being stabilized first. My only concern is that often a patient is prematurely diagnosed with anxiety or depression, or even substance-induced psychosis, and once again, rather than helping them work through what's causing their symptoms, the symptoms are medicated, which keeps them stuck in their pain instead of healing it.

In any case, after detox, psychiatrists and physicians should never prescribe mood-altering drugs. The addict is prone to take any mood-altering medication offered, so prescribing it only expands the addict's repertoire of drugs. To an addict, a drug is a drug is a drug, and once the substance is in the brain, the cycle resumes. More cheese, please.

> **To an addict, a drug is a drug is a drug.**

A final note about medication and children. Many teens in addiction treatment were put on Ritalin or Adderall as children. These drugs are stimulants used to treat psychiatric symptoms such as attention-deficit / hyperactivity disorder, obsessive-compulsive disorder, sleep disorders, aggression, anxiety, depression, and bipolar disorder. Regardless of whether the medication works or not, some children become addicted.[10]

The trend of putting children on medications that could permanently alter their brain's natural ability to regulate itself is alarming indeed. Some researchers have warned about the adverse effects of medicating children and have indicated family therapy should be the recommended treatment.[11]

It seems foolhardy to me to mess with a kid's brain while it is still developing, then expect it to be able to operate in a normal fashion. Kids who are hyper, compulsive, and depressed often are sent to school having eaten sugar-laden, processed foods (or nothing) for breakfast, are rushed to school by a stressed-out parent, or are exposed to trauma at school, home, or elsewhere—or all of the above. To put a child on medication without exhausting all other alternatives teaches the child that the defect is in them and a pill will fix everything—the perfect formula for future addiction. Proper diet can reduce many symptoms of attention-deficit / hyperactivity disorder.[12] Medicating a child should be used only as a last resort and only with the child's thorough understanding that it's a medical problem and not a personal defect.

Harm Reduction

Medically assisted treatment (MAT) is offered when a person fails at numerous attempts in treatment. Patients are prescribed drugs from which they are supposed to be titrated (weaned off), along with counseling and attendance at recovery meetings. Methadone, Suboxone, and naltrexone are prescribed for opiate addiction. Women who are opiate addicts and pregnant are administered methadone to prevent mother and fetal withdrawal and buprenorphine to reduce cravings for all opioids including morphine and heroin.[13] Chantix is prescribed for smoking cessation, and nicotine replacement therapy (NRT) is administered as an alternative to smoking. Naltrexone, which reduces the euphoric effects of alcohol, is also given to alcoholics so they can drink without craving more.

Huh? If you're taken aback after reading the above paragraph, you're not alone. It seems the benefits and the costs of using drugs to treat drugs may not be in the best interests of so many. If medication helps prevent a baby from going through withdrawal, it makes sense, but I've seen too many pregnant mothers stay on Suboxone after pregnancy. It seems it would be better for the baby to keep mom in treatment instead of on drugs so that at least the baby develops a healthy brain.

In general, I'm not sure why giving up on a program of abstinence is a good idea. There is the assumption that it's just too hard for the addict to stop rather than looking more carefully at the relapse triggers and responses. Giving additional dangerous drugs to people so they can better manage their drug use seems to be just another way to keep people addicted. Many MAT patients do not seek counseling or recovery meetings and are not weaned off the drugs, which is another shortcoming of this program.

This harm reduction method is based on the notion that addicts should be given drugs to reduce the negative consequences of using. Rather than trying to force abstinence or wean the addict, the drug abuser is provided the substances needed to prevent illicit drug use, overdose, spread of infectious diseases, and other harmful outcomes. Methadone is prescribed for heroin and other opiate addicts, and needle facilities are provided as well.

We should also be mindful of the risks involved and the possibility of overdose.[14] People in these programs are unlikely to recover because they are being given the subliminal message that they should *give up* trying to stop. If someone wants to commit their life to addiction, it's better they have the legal means to do so; it's physically and legally safer. However, there should be ample warning of the risks involved, the guidelines should be enforced rather than an unlimited supply provided, and the alternatives (recovery) should always be readily available. We shouldn't give up on anyone.

Another grave concern I have about MAT has come about recently. Several new patients have come to see me and reported that even though they'd been in AA and maintained sobriety for a long time, they are now smoking pot. They have reported being effortlessly prescribed a license to receive medical marijuana (in Florida) and have surrendered their recovery to relapse on pot. One patient who was thinking about smoking it told me it was a "gray area," and he received clarification when I told him it was not a gray area; you're either sober or you're not.

The form of marijuana that was legally approved in Florida for genuine medical conditions, such as pain control and reducing nausea from chemotherapy, is supposed to have minimal amounts of THC 0.8 percent or less so that it is not mood-altering.[15] Unfortunately, I've heard all too often that medical marijuana precipitated a relapse. Former alcoholics in recovery got hooked on it when it was prescribed as pain medication. The dozens of former pot smokers (who were in recovery) that I have spoken with who are on "medical marijuana" today say, "It's the best pot I've ever had."

Lots of people in Alcoholics Anonymous (AA) are now smoking pot under the illusion that they are sober. All the people who have come to see me are in the throes of an emotional crash. They have suffered numerous consequences, including having traumatized their children. It's clear to see that none of these people had been cured of their addiction in the first place or they would not have taken such risks.

My big beef with medically assisted treatment is that it's becoming compulsory, mandated by insurance companies that, for example, won't pay for treatment of drug addiction unless a patient is put on Suboxone. Some MAT facilities are going out into the community and recruiting potential patients for a fee (patient brokering), including homeless people, to get more government funding, and the few who are caught are often convicted of fraud.[16]

While it is important to respect a person's right to do what they want with their bodies, I'm not sure why providing legal drugs to a drug addict is considered treatment and not enabling. Giving drugs to addicts is just another way of lowering the bar and helping them use drugs—instead of helping them to recover. Yes, it's certainly better for a person to be legally administered a controlled substance if it helps them lead a relatively functional life rather than winding up in jail, being homeless, or contracting a disease. Drug addiction treatment is much less expensive than its alternatives, such as incarcerating addicted persons, and treatment doesn't isolate the person from their family.[17] I also agree that it is good to eliminate all criminal elements of drug addiction, but if that's the route we're going to take, why not legalize all drugs, tax them, and use the funds for education and prevention? We could start with teaching parents to lead by example and teach their children it is never a good idea to poison their precious, lovable bodies and developing brains with deadly substances.

Treatment Centers / Rehab

Up until the mid-1900s, people suffering from alcoholism or drug addiction were sent to asylums, but once released from the hospital, they usually relapsed. Though there aren't many records available tracking the length of time between sobering up and relapsing, we can gauge that it wasn't very long, as there were no preventive procedures available until AA came along.

When AA was founded, a recovering alcoholic would be called to the asylum or hospital to help the patient understand their addiction to alcohol, show them how to stop, and offer ongoing support in the form of personal contact and meetings. Once successful, the newly sober person would pass it on by helping others who were also suffering from alcoholism.

Over the past thirty years, treatment centers have become the go-to place for people who need help for an addiction. There are treatment centers for every possible addiction—most mood-altering substances, food, gambling, sex, codependency, and so forth. There are more than fourteen thousand treatment centers in the United States, pulling in annual revenue of $42 billion in 2020 and increasing.[18] Patients may go to treatment voluntarily, through a court order, or as a result of a family intervention.

Many treatment centers follow AA's 12-Step (or similar) model, including education about the signs and symptoms of addiction, evaluation for medication, counseling, exercise, meditation, family education, and aftercare. Treatment can be outpatient or inpatient and may range from thirty days up to a year or two. It is estimated that more than 65 to 70 percent of individuals relapse within 90 days following treatment.[19]

Many treatment centers are staffed with a team having varied amounts of training and differing views than the referring therapist. On far too many occasions, staff have changed the plan and made referrals to other therapists or agencies, creating another "dysfunctional family" scenario. When a referring therapist sends a patient to treatment, a collaborative effort is necessary to ensure the patient's safety and continuing treatment after discharge. This means having a sustainable support system in place prior to discharge, and a few hours of aftercare and one therapy session a week won't cut it.

Some facilities have inadequate staffing (psychiatrists, licensed experienced psychotherapists) and the treatment team can overstep the limits of their capabilities. Most addiction counselors and treatment centers define addiction as the insanity of doing the same thing again and again and expecting different results, but that is precisely what they are doing when they offer the patient the same failed treatment plan again and again and expect different results. When a facility continues to have the same patient with the same addiction and the same treatment, they are following their own definition of insanity. This presents a huge financial burden on patients and insurance companies, but even worse, it increases the patient's likelihood of failure and their sense of hopelessness. It's one thing to go to a few meetings and relapse, but it's emotionally devastating to spend a month or more of your life and, in many cases, invest upward of tens of thousands of dollars in treatment at a facility and fail. Also, since Alcoholics Anonymous, outpatient, and inpatient programs can't accurately track how many people stay sober and how many people relapse, there's not much data to support that residential treatment is any better than outside help such as AA or other nonresidential programs. If a patient can't stay sober in outpatient treatment, I'm all for residential, but if residential didn't work the first time, plan B should be different than plan A, like long-term detox or daily therapy combined with a sober-living facility if necessary.

One key reason for the immense relapse rate is that treatment centers tend to ignore that addicts usually don't remain in one addictive pattern. To cease one addictive behavior is like swatting a mosquito—it doesn't abolish all insects once and for all. It's more like the Whac-A-Mole game. You smash your addiction to alcohol, but next thing you know, another addiction— perhaps caffeine or cigarettes—has popped up. A maze is a maze is a maze.

It's not unusual for a person in treatment to smoke like a chimney, drink ten cups of coffee a day, or dive into love or sex addiction while being treated for alcoholism or drug abuse—right at the facility. Treatment generally focuses on one specific behavior and fails to recognize that all addictive behaviors exist for one reason—to get rid of unwanted feelings or obtain a more positive state of mind. This approach comes from a reluctance to separate the addict from all their vices at once.

> To cease one addictive behavior is like swatting
> a mosquito—it doesn't abolish all insects
> once and for all.

"First things first" is the standard. Best that the addict doesn't feel overwhelmed. But what I've found both in my practice and my personal experience is that no one can get completely well unless they first become unglued, then put back together, and there is no better place to do this than in treatment.

Disconnecting from the addictive pattern itself means stopping all the false comforts of substitute addictions and going right to the source. Healing from within is the only way to true freedom. More on this to come.

I recommend inpatient treatment only when it's in the patient's best interest to be removed from an unsafe environment or other methods of abstinence have failed. I carefully recommend a facility that is local, so the patient has a support system on departure, and also, one that will collaborate on and follow through with the patient's aftercare plan.

> I've never seen anyone control their addiction for very long. The fact that they've lost control is what defines their addicted status.

Behavior Modification

I'm not going to bother reviewing all the different types of behavior modification programs that have failed (such as "controlled drinking"). Typically, controlled use is measured intake. The patient keeps a chart of agreed-upon usage and is positively reinforced (intrinsically or otherwise) by sticking to that agreement.

Another method of behavior modification is aversion therapy, a highly controversial method of treatment that pairs a negative stimulus with the addiction of choice. For example, patients are shown pictures of a skull and crossbones next to a bottle of alcohol or given a mild electric charge every time they see a drink. Of course, every addict has already experienced enough negative jolts and it hasn't stopped them from drinking; it's only created a greater need to continue self-medicating.

I've worked with thousands of people who were addicted, and I've never seen anyone control their addiction for very long. The fact that they've lost control is what defines their addicted status. If a gambler could bet five dollars and walk away, she'd have accomplished that on her own. If a porn addict could control himself, he would have stopped before he got fired for using porn at work. Attempting to control any uncontrollable behavior is like teaching the mouse to have a little bite of the cheese, leave it, and make its way out of the maze.

The two most commonly used and effective methods for behavior modification are cognitive therapy and 12-Step programs.

Cognitive Therapy

Cognitive therapy helps people change their thoughts and regulate their feelings, so they can change the behavior that is triggered by those thoughts and feelings.

Rational Emotive Therapy

Rational emotive behavior therapy (REBT), developed by Dr. Albert Ellis, and other cognitive therapies are commonly used to treat addiction by teaching patients how to recognize that their unpleasant thoughts produce unpleasant feelings. By reorganizing the irrational beliefs and replacing them with more rational thoughts, feelings improve and thus remove the need to self-medicate. Cognitive therapy is an effective way to help people become more rational and be better thinkers, but it does not heal the wounds underneath the addiction, so it does not provide a cure. "If a bad feeling activates my addiction, I can rethink my way into a better feeling, and I won't want to act out," says the patient. *This might work for ripples of emotions, but not for the tidal waves.*

SMART Recovery

Self-Management and Recovery Training (SMART) is also a cognitive-based treatment to manage thoughts and feelings that addresses motivation, urges to use, and a balanced life. The group meetings are held once or twice weekly, in person or online, have a trained group facilitator, and are free of charge. A downside of SMART Recovery is that the one or two weekly meetings may not be enough for people whose addiction is constantly gnawing at them.

While cognitive therapy is a good adjunct tool for abstinence, it is not the end-all treatment. When a person attempts to cover an unhealed wound with cognitive behavioral techniques, it is like putting pink frosting on a mud pie. The unhealed wound festers, the addictive behavior either resumes in its original form or shapeshifts into a new drug of choice, and the person becomes sucked back into the maze. Cognitive therapy is a good first step at stopping an addiction, if followed by the necessary steps to heal the underlying wound.

> Cognitive therapy is an effective way to help people become more rational and be better thinkers, but it does not heal the wounds underneath the addiction, so it does not provide a cure.

12-Step Programs

The original 12-Step program of Alcoholics Anonymous was founded in 1935 when a few people, having gone through every imaginable attempt at sobriety, maintained abstinence through a behavioral and spiritual program that involved the admission of powerlessness, willingness to be abstinent, righting their wrongs, and finding a connection to a higher power, as outlined in the twelve steps of the program. AA views alcoholism as a mental obsession, physical addiction, and spiritual void.[20] From my observations, asking a higher power for help with addiction is extremely successful for those who follow this suggestion.

Since the first AA meeting, 12-Step meetings have popped up worldwide for every addiction imaginable. Attended by millions, meetings are ubiquitous—live or online—and cost nothing. In my opinion, the 12-Step program, when followed, is more effective for obtaining abstinence than any other form of treatment. Recent research has concluded that spiritual and religious-based interventions are more effective at reducing or eliminating substance use and are equally as effective as other programs on broader measures of wellness and function.[21]

AA reports a 50 percent success rate, with about 25 percent of the successes occurring after numerous attempts, though many of these folks may continue to go on and off the wagon.[22] These stats were probably accurate when members totaled a few thousand, but with millions trying AA, the percentage is probably less. But at least there are no costs or insurance requirements before care is offered.

The 12 Steps are an excellent way to stop a behavior and develop a solid support system, but the program falls short when it comes to addressing the trauma that underlies most addictive behavior. When asked to do a moral inventory and find "your own role" in painful relationships, it is unlikely that many uncover or address the original wound that led to the whole mess in the first place. Children are not the cause of their own abuse or neglect. Glossing over the pain only drives the memory of trauma deeper into the unconscious mind. People with unhealed childhood wounds tend to suffer chronic relapses, become addicted to something else, or continue to suffer.[23]

The 12-Step programs do recommend outside help for people who suffer emotional or mental disorders. In my opinion, that would be almost every addict.

Outpatient Psychotherapy

Many types of professionals offer outpatient psychotherapy; each has benefits as well as limitations.

Psychiatrists

Psychiatrists are medical doctors who specialize in psychiatry and who tend to treat most psychiatric disorders with medication. Unlike the founders of psychotherapy, Sigmund Freud and his followers, most psychiatrists today do not offer psychotherapy. When treating addiction, many psychiatrists write prescriptions to help patients reduce the withdrawal effects or substitute one drug for a less addictive one, or they prescribe Antabuse, which causes violent nausea when mixed with alcohol. A psychiatrist also will screen for a psychiatric diagnosis other than the addiction. I carefully select the psychiatrists with whom I work, so we can collaborate on treatment. I will cover this in greater detail later.

Psychologists

Psychologists have doctorate degrees in psychology, and counselors have master's degrees in mental health, psychology, or a related field such as social work. None are specifically trained in addictions, nor can they prescribe medication. I have seen numerous patients who were substance abusers and went to a psychologist or mental health counselor or both for years who knew little to nothing about the symptoms of addiction, so it was never addressed.

Addiction Counselors

Addiction counselors usually have either two-year or four-year degrees in addiction and are either certified or licensed in that field. The complexity of sorting out pathology from addiction is not a simple matter. Addiction counselors are trained to diagnose and counsel people on how to stay sober. They are not trained to diagnose or treat personality disorders: narcissism or borderline, antisocial, or paranoid personalities. Nor are they trained to treat mental illness, such as schizophrenia, manic depression, major depressive disorders, or psychosis, all of which require that the patient be on medication to be able to perform life's daily tasks and functions.

Addiction counselors are not trained to discern the difference between an organic psychosis and a drug-induced psychosis. Research has indicated a link between young pot users and an increased risk for schizophrenia-like symptoms.[24] I have treated several young men who were diagnosed with schizophrenia, but who were in fact addicted to marijuana, and when they stopped using, the schizophrenic symptoms stopped. This misdiagnosis is common, and these types of situations require a psychiatrist's evaluation to be sure.

As one example, John was brought to therapy by his uncle because he was "acting strange." John had been talking about aliens and was writing nonsensical things in his notebook. He also thought he was a unique species of human who could breathe underneath water. All of these are schizophrenic-like symptoms, but John had had no prior episodes of psychosis.

However, John had used large quantities of both marijuana and hallucinogens. He reported, and his uncle confirmed, that he had been in AA for six months, and yet he was psychotic. John's symptoms were inexplicable, and I referred him to the psychiatrist with whom I consult and who is a highly skilled diagnostician. He was unsure whether John's psychosis was organic or the result of drug use, but he prescribed him the appropriate medication, so John could be stabilized. After six months, John was weaned off the medication to see if his symptoms would return. When they did not, we were able to draw the conclusion that his symptoms were most likely due to his prior drug use. To be on the safe side, John continued to meet with the psychiatrist every few months.

Psychoanalysts

Psychoanalysts are either licensed in psychiatry, psychology, or mental health and are required to complete several years of postgraduate education, supervision, and personal psychoanalysis. Treatment addresses the underlying causes of emotional disorders, and psychoanalysts must go through their own personal psychoanalysis before certification—at least three or more sessions per week for usually a minimum of four years. Other than psychoanalysts, I've heard of no other licensed professionals who are required to have had therapy prior to certification. This would be similar to a nutritionist who doesn't eat healthy food or a heart surgeon who smokes. When therapists have not done the theraputic work on themselves that they are performing on others, they could conceivably be unhealthier than the people they are treating, and not as equipped to provide the right advice.

I've often worked with people who suffered undiagnosed addiction, and prior to seeing me, were in psychoanalysis for years. These patients might have connected the dots of the precipitating factors of their addiction (childhood trauma), but if they were still actively using they were unable to access the emotions that must be grieved to heal. Even therapists who are highly skilled (but not trained in addictions) might not see addiction when it is right in front of them.

Psychotherapists

Psychotherapists can include all of the above and also include licensed clinical social workers; mental health, pastoral, and marriage and family counselors; psychopharmacologists; and psychiatric nurse practitioners. These individuals have graduate degrees and meet additional training criteria to be licensed.

Sober coaches

Sober coaches are certified in coaching a particular behavior. Their fees are usually more affordable, and insurance will not cover their services. Sober coaches help clients achieve specific goals to facility sobriety.

Confused? Welcome to my world. I haven't even introduced the other types of licensed or certified addiction professionals: educational psychologists, guidance counselors, hypnotherapists, sponsors, all with varying degrees of education and training in addiction diagnosis and treatment. All are well-meaning and all have their own opinions that, in many cases, are commonly offered to the same patient. With all the conflicting advice and variations in diagnosis, it is no wonder that people struggling with addiction are in a maze. I ran around in the maze a long time before I was able to put it all together.

4

WHY TREATMENT FAILS

Failure is not a single, cataclysmic event. . . . Failure is nothing
more than a few errors in judgment repeated every day.
—Jim Rohn

It takes a family. According to the National Institute on Drug Abuse, the relapse rate for people who go to treatment (alcohol, nicotine, weight, illicit drug abuse) is about 85 percent within a year.[1] In other words, treatment is not as good as those who attend 12-Step meetings without other interventions.[2] It is difficult to track the actual rates of most individuals because Alcoholics Anonymous (AA) does not keep records, and regardless of the type of treatment, it's not uncommon for someone to have difficulty stopping the addictive behavior on the first attempt. Addiction is synonymous with isolation; there must be a caring support system in place for long-term sobriety. Without a fulfilling life and healthy bonding, the addict will go back to the maze.

One reason for this is that when people leave treatment, often they return to the same environment with the same enablers or active addicts or both. Patients discharged to unsupportive environments are likely to relapse. This is why I believe it is useless to treat an addict without the whole family having treatment as well. It is a difficult adjustment for an addict to be stone sober or otherwise abstinent from addictions and return to the same dysfunctional household. It is painful for a patient to get sober, then reunite with a partner who thinks things will automatically improve. They won't, and both people need help. An adolescent who returns to the same dysfunctional family where the pain began will suffer and is virtually certain to relapse.

Judith brought her son, Randy, to therapy because, after several residential treatments and two years of sobriety, he had relapsed. In the session, Randy reported to me that he'd been sexually abused in his early childhood, and his brother had died of an overdose six months prior.

> Addiction is synonymous with isolation; there must be a caring support system in place for long-term sobriety.

During that initial interview, it was clear to me that even though Judith had brought her son to therapy, she was emotionally disconnected from the seriousness of her son's condition. Randy repeatedly said he needed help, and he knew he was relapsing because of the sexual abuse. It was painful to witness Judith's lack of interest in this traumatic experience that Randy clearly wanted to discuss. Judith never asked him who had sexually abused him or when. When I asked Randy if he wanted to talk about it, he agreed to come back for another session. I spent the remainder of the first session stressing to both of them the importance of immediate and intensive therapy, especially since the combination of Randy having lost a brother to an overdose and being sexually abused put him at an exceptionally high risk.

However, when I asked to see Randy the next day, neither Randy nor his mother thought it necessary to return so soon. When he missed his appointment the following Monday and did not return my calls, I contacted his mother. She told me he was sleeping. I stressed the urgency of seeing him soon, and Judith said she'd tell him. Neither of them ever called back, and they ignored my calls, so I had to let it go.

Since Randy was an adult, I could not get help from Child Protective Services, and since he was not overtly suicidal, I could not have him committed. I could only feel appalled and pained that Randy might become another overdose statistic—that his mother might lose another son—and there seemed nothing she was going to do to stop it.

Though it's difficult to stay sober in a dysfunctional family, it's not impossible. I always tell patients they can be the one to place the mark *Addiction Stops Here* in their family tree.

Families aren't the only threat to recovery. Physicians can often be the cause of relapse. One patient, Dean, while being scheduled to have knee replacement surgery, was prescribed ninety doses of OxyContin for postsurgical pain. He explained to his doctor that he was in recovery and could not take narcotics. The surgeon's nurse told him that he had to take the pills and specifically, "You have to stay in front of the pain or you will get addicted." When he tried to explain to her that he was already addicted to all mood-altering substances, she told him, "If you don't take the medication, you won't be able to do the physical therapy and won't heal properly."

Denial is the primary defense mechanism that keeps the addict going.

That's all Dean needed to hear; after all, the doctor knows best. I could not convince Dean to follow the protocol for recovering addicts, which is to have someone else administer the dose as prescribed and, as soon as possible, switch to a nonnarcotic pain reliever. By the time Dean came back to therapy, he'd finished the first ninety pills and had filled a second prescription. Two years later, he was still on the same dosage of one pill every four hours. Thankfully, Dean stayed in therapy and was finally able to get detoxed from the OxyContin and back into recovery. I have seen dozens of cases where physicians have sabotaged a person's recovery, and I find it bordering on criminal negligence. For anyone interested in learning more about this type of protocol, I'd recommend you read books or watch miniseries and documentaries that explain the opioid crisis and the long-term consequences of OxyContin. Physicians should take heed of their patients' addiction history, prescribe a limited dose, and be sure there is someone to administer the meds.

As previously mentioned, unknowing therapists are also a significant contributor to relapse. Alarming as it is, therapists often make the error of telling a patient in recovery that they are not an addict or alcoholic. Denial is the primary defense mechanism that keeps the addict going. When the professional is also in denial and tells a recovering person that they are not addicted, the relapse wheels are set in motion. Even my own psychoanalyst, with whom I spent thirteen years, repeatedly told me she did not think I was an alcoholic, even though I told her I'd been in recovery for many years prior to my analysis. She could not see beyond her own level of understanding. Like so many other therapists, her mental image of someone addicted to substances was more like a person you'd see on a television show, someone using around the clock or who has hit rock bottom. In reality, according to the National Institutes of Health, 20 percent of all alcoholics are high functioning.[3] If you add up all the people hooked on other types of legal and illegal drugs, the total number of highly functioning addicts will be much greater than just alcoholics. If we remember that addiction (like any illness) is progressive and that someone doesn't have to be homeless before they've contracted the disease, then we will do a better job of seeing it and treating it early on. No therapist should ever tell recovering patients they are not addicted.

When dual-diagnosed patients go off their psychotropic medication, relapse is likely. Believe it or not, many therapists tell patients they don't need to be on medication for psychosis. When someone sinks into a major depressive-suicidal episode, goes on a manic spending spree, thinks they can fly off a building or communicate with extraterrestrials or becomes otherwise psychotic, the therapist will quickly discover why the patient needs medication. Unfortunately, by then it is often too late, and the patient has resumed the addiction in an attempt to modulate their symptoms. A patient should never go off meds unless under the supervision of an addiction-trained psychiatrist.

Enablers are often the key catalysts of relapse. It is typical for a loved one to either consciously or unconsciously sabotage someone's recovery. I once treated a family where the mother constantly undermined her young son's recovery. In spite of all his behavior—drug dealing, binge drinking, a near-death experience, marijuana psychosis—she insisted on telling her son he did not have a problem. She refused to go to Al-Anon (the 12-Step program for loved ones of the addicted) or read any of the educational materials I provided. She even went so far as to encourage her son to have a "little drink" on his first AA anniversary and on his second one as well. Obliging his ill-intentioned mother, who was too frightened to face either the threat of her own possible dependency on alcohol or the threat of losing control over her son, he relapsed both times under her urging. Sadly, it is far too common that parents are unwilling to utilize resources they need to best help their children, and they often fail to realize this mistake until it is too late.

> Enablers are often the key catalysts of relapse.

In other families, food addicts are tempted with their favorite dishes, sex addicts are tempted with triggers such as a partner suggesting they watch porn, gamblers and work addicts are tempted by a family member who complains about financial lack. Enablers unconsciously sabotage the recovering person because the addict's recovery threatens the enablers' codependency. Someone who has been taking care of the addict may feel less needed, fear abandonment, or even feel resentful and threatened by the change and the loss of control. Sometimes they will go so far as to tell the newly sober person, "I liked you better when you were high," and the recovering addict is too miserable, raw, and vulnerable to remain resolute.

Wounded Healers

Wounded patients who don't receive proper care aren't the only problem. Another reason so many mental health professionals have been unable to treat addicted patients successfully is the failure to see their own addictions and unhealed wounds. I can personally attest that anything that isn't resolved will definitely become a problem in the therapy room. Supervision isn't enough; personal growth is a lifetime commitment.

I've known more therapists who were heavy drug and alcohol users than not. Many people are interested in the field of psychology because of their own childhood trauma, and they have empathy for other people who have suffered similar experiences. It's not enough to care about someone else; if you haven't taken the time or done the work to heal yourself, your ability to help anyone else is limited. The tendency to overlook traits in oneself that you can clearly see in others is far too common in the addiction treatment community. I've counseled many clinicians who thought they were "recovered" only to reveal they were beholden to various addictions, including addictive relationships, caffeine, gambling, pornography, sugar, Tinder hookups, video gaming, work, or anything else that would provide a source of superficial relief from their own emotional wounds.

Licensed psychiatrists and therapists must pass all sorts of tests to receive their qualifications but yet are never required to have their own psychological testing or be evaluated for possible addictions. Yet they are allowed to go out into their communities and work with the public. Our communities need therapists who are empowered role models, not addicts steeped in their own denial. If a patient is stuck in a maze, looking for a lever, it's not very likely that the therapist will be able to help them see the exit when they are stuck in the same maze. Patients cannot get well if the people helping them are not well. I often say kids can only be as healthy as their healthiest role model. The same is true of patients.

Sober versus Well

A person can stop an addiction and be sober and still suffer. A person can be sober for many years and still be as emotionally unhealthy as the first day of sobriety. Being well means that you have healed the underlying cause of the addiction and thus have removed the need to use anything or anyone to pacify relentless internal pain. Until addiction is treated as a symptom of the emotional damage it represents, it is unlikely the relapse rate will decline. Until we address the cause, the best we can hope for is to leave the recovering person discontent and unlikely to form the intimate bonds that are natural to those who are not only sober but who are also recovered from their emotional wounds.

Of all the reasons for relapse, the primary cause underlying the addiction itself is the originating wound that remains unhealed. When a child suffers trauma that remains unhealed, it needs constant soothing. Until that original wound is healed, the addiction will substitute temporary soothing for actual healing.

One Final Reason Treatment Fails— You Have to Want It

Now that we've explored all the external reasons, I would be remiss if I failed to mention that treatment is unlikely to be successful if you're not committed to changing your life. If you're not ready, no amount of perfection—the best meetings, sponsors, therapists, and treatment—will get you sober. Until you realize that you have sold yourself the lie that something or someone is worth continuing your self-destructive behaviors, you aren't ready. Once you understand who you really are and what your true value is, leaving the addiction won't be a struggle. More about this later.

Recap

To sum it all up, here's where we currently stand in the field of addictions: The experts lack a consensus on naming the illness and lack agreement on symptoms; thus, addictions often go undiagnosed. Failure to diagnose is arguably the greatest barrier to effective treatment. If you don't know you have it, it can't be treated.

When a proper diagnosis is made, the prescribed treatments include a broad range of options, including self-talk, 12-Step meetings, outpatient therapy, and long-term residential treatment, yet every one of these has a high rate of relapse. This is partly because the people assigned to treat addiction are not properly trained to do so. Also, as previously mentioned, treatment success is hindered when therapists are sicker than the patients and have yet to address or heal their own emotional wounds.

Another common block to successful treatment is that patients are not properly screened for dual diagnosis (i.e., identifying a mental illness or other addictive behaviors). As a result, conditions such as schizophrenia and manic depression, which require medication, go untreated. This blocks even the best trained mental health professional from being able to support the person in addiction recovery. Further, looking at only part of the picture makes it likely that the patient will fall into a complementary addictive behavior while they are in treatment for the primary one (for example, taking up caffeine, eating, smoking, or sex addiction while addressing alcohol or drug addiction). When patients aren't afforded the opportunity to address all their addictive behaviors simultaneously, it gravely inhibits any chance of long-term recovery.

Another common reason for the high failure rate is that patients are repeatedly sent back into the same environment in which they used in the first place. Some treatment centers are more concerned with bottom-line profit than what's best for the patient. Unless the entire support system is addressed, the patient is likely to relapse.

We need to change the way we are treating addiction. Under the current model, we aren't leading people out of the maze. We are merely adding more corridors.

Finally, the biggest reason that treatment fails is that the patient's underlying wound is never healed and the void replaced with self-love.

A Change in Perspective

It is not my intention or desire to attack the people who are treating addiction, or the models they use. We cannot blame the people who have tried to help. Nor should we blame the doctors, advertisers, drug dealers, or sales reps who sell our society on the idea that the solution to our unhappiness, our empty feelings, or whatever discomforts we experience can be found in a pill, a toke, a shot, a sports car, or any other distraction.

All in all, we've settled for something that makes us feel better in the moment rather than something that actually makes us better. We've settled for "getting relief" rather than being well. We've settled for "getting sober" over being happy and fulfilled.

Treating addiction can't be about doing the same thing while we watch people get sicker and even die. It can't be just about making money. We're talking about the tens of thousands of young kids who are dropping dead by the minute. We're talking about people who lose everything because they've gambled it away, spent it all on sex, or eaten themselves to death. We're talking about families who are broken, not because of incompatibility but due to an addiction. We're talking about people who never achieve their purposes here because their bodies and minds have been hijacked. We're talking about the fact that addiction is the world's biggest killer. If you get right down to it, almost all premature deaths are due to some type of addiction.

The time has come to take down the wall of pathological resistance and see the truth—that we have become a highly addicted society. We need to face the reality that we are addicted and that we remain addicted because we don't want to deal with our feelings. If we are ever to break free of addiction and reclaim our lives, we must each, as individuals, be willing to accept that the only way we can exit the maze is to address the real cause.

It's time to end the insanity. It's time we agree on a clear definition of addiction and create a treatment plan that works.

> **We need to face the reality that we are addicted and that we remain addicted because we don't want to deal with our feelings.**

The same authorities who provide the diagnosis criteria for addiction, but don't call it that, are the same authorities who say you can never be cured. Even if "once an addict, always an addict" is true, why should we stop there?

If you are struggling with addiction or suspect you might be, I want to show you a solution that goes beyond mere abstinence, that transcends the current diagnosis and treatment models. I'm inviting you to go beyond the need to reach outside yourself for something to make you feel better. I invite you to travel the path inward to a place where you can experience a sense of peace and contentment anytime you choose, a place that can never be attained through the pacifying substitutes you have accepted all your life.

This path can lead way beyond the idea of the "quick fix." It goes deeper than the strategy of using willpower to overcome cravings or to temper a constant state of need. But before you can give yourself that experience, we have to go into that place—the place that has made you feel you need a quick fix—and then find that place inside of you that can be cured.

It's time to get out of the maze for good. The easiest way to find a way out of the maze is to take a bird's-eye view, so you can see the whole picture. From that vantage, you can see where the exit is, and you can see a path to get there.

Here are a few questions to give you a better sense of where you might have gotten stuck and the things that haven't worked up to this point.

Self-Evaluation Questionnaire

Identify Your Level of Hope

1. Have you been trying to get help for a long time?
2. Do you feel like you've tried many different ways to feel better, but for some reason you're stuck?
3. Have you had therapy or are in recovery, but still feel like something's missing? Describe what you think was missing from your therapy as well as what might be missing in your commitment to getting better.
4. Have you lost faith in the therapy? If so, why?
5. Do you feel hopeless about ever getting better? If so, what would need to change for you to regain hope?
6. Did you read anything in Part 1 that specifically applies to you? If so, make a note of it.

PART 2

ONE CAUSE

Imagine you are a scientist standing over a maze with a mouse running through it. As you look down, right in the middle of the maze, you see a black hole. Around that black hole is a vortex. Everything that goes near the hole is sucked into the vortex, making it part of an ever-growing darkness. Light cannot enter or escape. The mouse is so busy searching for its reward, it doesn't notice the hole is growing. Nor is the mouse aware that, left unchecked, the entire maze and everything in it can be sucked into the hole.

Deep in the center of the black hole is where the cause of addiction resides. In these next chapters, we will enter the hole together, so you can see what's there and find a way out.

5

WHERE ADDICTION STARTS

Although it pains me to admit it, I am quite familiar with
the holes in life. And this familiarity is due to the fact that
I spend far more time in these holes than I spend on
the paths that brought me to them.
—Craig D. Lounsbrough, *Flecks of Gold on a Path of Stone*

I believe we're all born with a natural tendency toward happiness—to feel good in our own skin. Every newborn is hardwired for happiness and success given that their basic needs are met. It is the natural state of being human. Yet the fact of life is that trauma happens. Disappointment happens. Pain, sorrow, and loss happen. But no matter how brutal, awful, or intense the pain suffered, trauma itself does not cause addiction. Unaddressed trauma does. Unhealed emotional trauma becomes the wound that creates a persistent ache, pain, or craving that calls for relief. This is why so many of us turn to substances or activities that numb—we want to blot out that residual pain.

The residual pain of trauma (physical or emotional) is there because it was never dealt with on the emotional level. It got buried, so trauma seeps into our consciousness as a constant ache or an unshakable feeling of emptiness, a void that, despite repeated and misguided efforts, cannot be filled. Or at least it can seem that way.

When my patients first attempt to stop an addiction, they report the same feelings: "I feel hollow inside," "I feel like the wind blows through me," "I feel like an empty statue." Underlying all addictions is a battle—a person fighting intolerable feelings and attempting to fill a gnawing, persistent, invisible hole.

What few ever come to realize is that the pain or emptiness persists because it is acting as an alarm, attempting to tell us that our emotional heart has been bruised and needs attention. The empty feeling is asking us to turn inward and give ourselves more love. But instead, we douse ourselves with drugs and anything else that will distract but only reinjure us. These actions merely compound the trauma and intensify the feeling of emptiness. This is also why the deeper one goes into addiction, the greater the pain, the greater the emptiness—it's telling us that we're going in the wrong direction. I call it the invisible hole, because we can feel it all the time, but while we are caught in the maze of addiction, we can't see it.

A Hole to Fill

If you're addicted or suspect you are, know that long before you developed even an inkling that something like addiction could happen to you, you probably noticed a feeling of being disconnected from yourself or others—as if you were someone different or defective. When you were young, you might have felt you were born into the wrong family, since everyone seemed to fit in but you. You might have suffered abuse. Perhaps members of your family were unhappy, and you felt responsible for making everyone feel better, only to feel sad yourself when things did not improve. Maybe you were shy and spent hours alone, wondering why everyone had friends but you. Perhaps you had all the material things in life but were discontent. You might have craved affection and intimacy from distant, unaffectionate parents, causing you to seek that missing touch with people who hurt you or took advantage. Perhaps you lost a parent and felt depressed and alone, with no one to share your grief.

Whatever the original trauma, realize that, over time, the initial sense of unease grew and became what I call the invisible hole, a persistent, unrelenting sense of pain and emptiness that I believe is the driving force behind all manifestations of addiction. Regardless of the particular form or expression, if you look closely, you will see that addiction originates here. The invisible hole is the pain left by some unmet need or betrayal during your childhood.

Children are born completely helpless and dependent upon their caregivers for survival. Children are wired to seek a connection with and the approval of their parents. Because babies are totally dependent, any perceived lack of approval or insufficient nurturing can be viewed as a direct threat to their survival. No parenting is perfect, but if children are shown again and again that being loved is conditional and that they are not okay as they are, an invisible hole forms, and the child's psyche becomes vulnerable to addiction. It's not natural for a child to feel unlovable by their own parents.

> **The invisible hole is the pain left by some unmet need or betrayal during your childhood.**

It is my belief that a child who has a genetic predisposition to addiction is not doomed to become addicted unless they also experience trauma that goes untreated and unhealed. Many recovering alcoholics have educated their children about addiction, making them aware of the possibility that they may have a predisposition to developing an addiction. But in the absence of an unhealed trauma, no invisible hole will be formed, and without the invisible hole, addictive behaviors don't hold the same allure. If people feel whole and complete within themselves and notice that their actions look like addictive behavior, they'll stop. Or if they're really smart, knowing they have a genetic predisposition, they'll never start in the first place. They will recognize it's not good for them, and they will walk away unscathed.

Unfortunately, the combination of ineffective parenting strategies and growing up in an addicted society predisposes children to grow into addicted adults. Technology is priming children to be constantly distracted and to expect immediate gratification. The days of creativity, resting, playing outside, and learning how to wait for special treats are almost gone. How often have you seen an entire family on their phones while dining out? Communication during meals is a way to bond, learn about one another, and express different points of view. The child who learns these skills with their family will have confidence at future social events.

Children who grow up with addicted parents are more likely to emulate the behavior they observe. Often parents unwittingly model or encourage behavior that sets in motion ineffective coping strategies. A mother who consoles her troubled child with food teaches her child that food will make the hurt go away, and the child will grow up and seek food for comfort rather than soothing words and hugs.

Social programming also is a huge factor in setting up kids for addiction. From the time children start watching television, they see images of ways to "feel good": the extra-cheesy pizza is extra-cheesy festive; the little pill removes all worries and turns your frowny face into a smiley one; the sexy new car and the icy bottle of beer make you more desirable to hot men and women. All of these messages convey to impressionable minds that they need to get something from the outside to feel okay on the inside. Few advertisements convey that these are things to enjoy but are *not* here to complete us.

No one sets out to become an addict; it catches us off guard. An addiction can happen quickly or slowly and can affect anyone regardless of intelligence, social class, ethnic group, or religion. One cigarette a day becomes four, then becomes a pack or more. One drink a day becomes a few, then becomes a quart or more. A few extra pounds become ten, then fifty or more. If this reminds you of your experience, consider that you might also have thought you were in control at first, but all the while, you were already trapped. By the time you realized you had a problem, you were already in the maze.

"Next time will be different" was your motto as you swore off alcohol, porn, spending, or whatever else lured you in. Time and time again, no amount of guilt ever reformed you; it only took you further down. In fact, that voice that makes you feel guilty is the same voice that talked you into relapsing in the first place.

You convinced yourself your "bad habits" had nothing to do with lost loves, careers, or people who betrayed you. As everything you valued in life slipped through your fingers, you might have still thought you had control. If any of this sounds familiar, embrace that awareness. There's no need to feel ashamed. This is a common scenario, and it can happen to anyone.

I have a dear friend, an Ivy League graduate who lost his medical practice and his wife to alcohol. Later, after getting sober, he started a new life at a state university, doing research. But he began to drink again. He's been arrested twice, once for driving his car into a building and once for threatening to shoot his former colleague and friend. But he still thought he was in control, even as his addiction was consuming him once again. As I write this, he still has not sought help. I hope he does, but I fear that he, like so many others, has been digested by the disease.

Some manifestations of addiction are more socially acceptable than others; some are uglier, messier, or more violent, but they all serve the same purpose. A person who chews gum incessantly might not be viewed the same way as a person who suffers from debilitating drug dependence. But in all cases, addicts who are not satisfying their urges will suffer emotional stress—anger, agitation, moodiness—until their cravings are met. We all recognize that taking away someone's cigarettes or booze will make them anxious, upset, and moody. But try taking chewing gum from someone who uses it for oral gratification or asking a compulsively neat person to leave the house messy for a whole day and see what happens. You will observe the same anxiety, anger, and discontent. Regardless of which pacifier they use, addicts will experience similar emotional withdrawal symptoms in one form or another because each is using their drug of choice in an attempt to fill the same invisible hole.

> **Regardless of the form it takes,
> there is only one addiction.**

The guy driving his Rolls-Royce might not see he's in the same addiction hole when he pulls up next to someone strung out on drugs holding a sign that reads "Will Work for Food." But if the luxury car owner has just come off an eighty-hour workweek and is on his way to the nearest strip club for a night of boozing and lap dances, he might indeed be embroiled in exactly the same struggle—same disease, different costumes.

Regardless of the form it takes, there is only one addiction, and it always comes from the same urge to fill that imaginary hole—the one formed in that moment in time when a person suffers a hurt that leaves them with a feeling of being less than, of being unlovable, of not being enough, of feeling worthless, then tried to cover up or fill the hole left by that pain with something that would make it go away. But that hole cannot be filled with drugs or booze or sex or work. And addiction can't be solved by mere abstinence either.

Why Abstinence Fails

Abstinence is an excellent place to start the healing process, but the person who is attempting to recover from addiction through abstinence likely will find they've underestimated its versatility. For example, if you were ever a smoker, you might think that by giving up cigarettes, you gave up your addiction, but think again. Did you take up chewing gum? Sucking on Jolly Ranchers? Eating? What new behavior did you pick up to offset or distract you from your cravings?

Addiction is a signal from your unconscious that there is a deep hurt inside you needing to be healed. The goal is to get you to heal. And it is not going to give up trying to get your attention just because you gave up your first-choice distraction. Until the wound is healed, addiction will continue to morph itself and resurface in another form, like the trick a magician plays of hiding an object under one of three cups, and you can never guess which one. Addiction is the object that appears to have magically shifted around. The object is always there, but you never know where it will pop up next.

Regardless of the form, driven by the same unresolved pain, addiction offers the illusion that the empty feeling has disappeared—temporarily, at least. We get lured in, looking for the right fix—a few drinks, a joint, a container of ice cream, a new relationship. When we look to people, places, and things as ways to fill the invisible hole, we remain in the maze.

Rather than focus on the specific behavior, the best way to know if you're addicted is to do a gut check to see how you feel when you are not using. You might feel as if you are floating in a place of nothingness or that you don't even know yourself anymore. You might feel that you are invisible, and no one sees you. You might feel dead inside, and your diminishing life spark can be ignited only with the next drink or drug dose. You might feel that your addiction is the only thing you can look forward to in your desolate, solitary life. You might have spent years in recovery meetings and still wonder why you are not happy. You might be haunted by a persistent feeling of inauthenticity.

Clyde told me he couldn't figure out why he still felt like something was wrong with him after ten years of sobriety and therapy. "I don't understand why I feel like there's something wrong inside of me. How can I feel so fake when I've done so much to get better? I didn't feel this strange when I was using."

> **Addiction offers the illusion that the empty feeling has disappeared—temporarily, at least.**

Clyde had been in five different relationships during his ten years sober, and they all held the same pattern. He would get involved with people he knew weren't right for him and were unlikely to last. Then, he'd get bored and end the relationship after about a year. Even though he'd had therapy and wasn't drinking or drugging, he still had not healed the hole that was driving him into unfulfilling relationships—untreated addiction. He was getting an endorphin high from the newness, but once that faded, so did his desire. Clyde had to explore the shame that bound him in low self-esteem and robbed him of what he truly felt and wanted. He decided to be alone and face the feelings that drove him into unsatisfactory relationships. He often wanted to stop therapy but persevered and worked through his internal conflicts with intimacy, finding his voice, sharing his vulnerabilities, and standing alone. He was then able to feel comfortable in his own skin and stop using women to cover up his feelings of inadequacy.

The Way Out

When we're addicted, it's as though we walk around holding a cord looking for the next place to plug in and fill up. Hypnotized into believing that somehow "garbage in" will fill the invisible hole, we keep searching the garbage can for the next quick fix—rather than trying to understand how the hole got there in the first place. Believing that toxins, poisons, and super thrills are fun and good for us, we are oblivious to all the warning signs. We are addicted before we ever realize that the only thing we accomplish by "indulging" in all these distractions is expanding the vortex of pain. And the only reason that discomfort exists is to point out that we have a wound, and we need to heal it.

Even if you are in recovery and you are still unhappy, I want you to know that there is hope. There is one way out.

There is only one way out of the maze of addiction, and it's not to be found on the other side at the perimeter. The idea that you can exit the maze at the same place you entered is an illusion—and it will cause you to reenact the trauma that put you there.

The invisible hole that represents the lifetime of painful experiences must be faced. If you want to heal, you must go into the center and enter the vortex, where the root of all your pain and trauma resides.

Just as Luke Skywalker had to go into the swamp and face the demons of his past before Yoda could help him gather his power in *The Empire Strikes Back*, you, too, must go into your painful past and penetrate the wound before you can fully heal and find your true power. I'm not going to lie—it is an uncomfortable process. But by choosing to love yourself over and over, you can overcome the fear of facing your demons. The following chapters will explain how you can lead yourself out of that nightmare and into a place of fearless love for yourself and others.

Self-Evaluation Questionnaire

Identify Ways You've Tried to Fill the Hole

1. Do you remember the first time you felt an uneasiness inside you that you wanted to rid yourself of? Describe that experience.
2. When was the first time you turned to something you knew was "bad" (alcohol, cigarettes, sugar, and so forth) for "comfort"? What were the circumstances? What did you take? How did it make you feel?
3. What happened after you experienced that first sense of relief from using?
4. Did you soon look forward to the next time? Did the uneasiness and feeling of discontent return? If so, describe what it felt like.
5. Did you notice that the more you tried to fill the empty feeling, the bigger it grew? If so, describe what happened.
6. List all the ways you tried to fill the hole.
7. Has the hole gone away? How do you know? If it's still there, how does it feel?
8. Name all the actions or substances you have used to avoid facing emotional pain.

9. Describe how you felt after you used and the high wore off.
10. Describe what it would feel like to be free of a behavior you'd like to stop.
11. Once the wounds in the invisible hole are healed, what do you want to have in that space?
12. How would it feel to have that void inside of you filled with joy, peace, and contentment?

HOW THE HOLE BEGAN

There are wounds that never show on the body that are deeper
and more hurtful than anything that bleeds.
—**Laurell K. Hamilton,** *Mistral's Kiss*

Before we observe how the hole forms in the psyche, we'll need to
gain a clear picture of the conditions that create solid self-esteem in
a child—the type of personality that has no predisposition to addiction.

First, let's take another look at rodents. Since rats are social in nature
and have brains that function similarly to a human's, they are often used
in experiments to understand human behavior. Both are social, warm-
blooded mammals that respond similarly to situations. In a famous study
called the Rat Park experiment, Bruce Alexander and colleagues per-
formed an experiment to determine if rats would find highly addictive
drugs "irresistible."[1]

The scientists discovered that rats raised in a large box (communal
park) with plenty of food, activities, and other rats to play with showed little
to no interest in consuming (highly addictive) morphine. These findings
were compared with a prior experiment in which rats were kept in solitary
confinement in small metal cages. When morphine was offered to these
rats, they consumed high doses. These results debunked the hypothesis that
highly addictive drugs are the problem, because the rats in the park who
had all their needs met, including social ones, showed little to no interest in
saturating their brains with a mood-altering substance. The results demonstrated that loneliness and lack are the drivers of drug abuse, not the drug
itself. Similarly, a child who feels fulfilled will not be susceptible to substitutes for fulfilling experiences—there's no hole to fill.

Ideally, before a baby is conceived, two people who are in love and
ready to have a child start to prepare for a new life before the pregnancy

ever occurs. They are emotionally and financially stable and feel confident that they are ready to take on the responsibility of childcare (in some cases, it might be a single parent with help) that will span at least two decades. Of course, families have various levels of income, and not all children grow up with financial security. Money is not a requirement to raise a child who feels confident, loved, and lovable.

Also, today, there are many different types of parenting models (same-sex, trans-sex, surrogate, single) who can meet the baby's needs just as effectively as traditional, heterosexual parenting. The important factors are the key elements outlined below which need not be determined by sexual orientation but more importantly, by parenting that makes a baby feel loved and secure.

Before pregnancy, the mother makes sure she is healthy and fit, so her body can properly house and nourish a developing fetus. During pregnancy, the mother's priority is taking care of the fetus: getting enough rest, eating healthy food, and experiencing minimal stress. She does not drink, smoke, or otherwise put toxins in her body.

The childbirth is as natural as possible without putting mother or child at risk, with both parents present. The baby is promptly handed over to the mother, who cradles her child and looks into the baby's eyes, while an outpouring of love flows down from both parents. They tell the baby, "We love you; we are so happy you are here."

Again, ideally, the mother breastfeeds so her baby gets the antibodies, colostrum, prebiotics, and other health benefits that are not available in formula.

The baby is brought home to a secure environment, and the mother continues to bond with her child. Her attention is focused on the baby, and she adapts her life to the infant's needs. The child basks in the warmth of the mother's body during feedings, and her primary focus is attuning herself to her baby. The father also bonds with the child by participating as much as possible in the child's care. This baby feels safe, warm, full, and secure. Ideally, extended family members—grandparents, aunts, uncles, and so forth, who also provide additional support to the parents—are healthy, balanced individuals adding greater security to the family bond. As the infant grows, the parents continue to adjust to the child's needs, yet they make sure they remain intimate and connected as a couple. Their world rotates around proper care of their offspring, including an environment that stimulates the child's natural curiosity. Advances such as first steps are met with approval and delight. When the infant starts to assert independence, the parents are supportive, teaching the child to be confident, that it's safe to break away as a separate person while continuing to receive support.

As the child grows, the parents teach healthy habits of self-care, such as good nutrition, obtaining appropriate mental stimulation, and exercise. Natural talents are cultivated and encouraged. The parents take the time to explain why these things are important to the body and mind, so the child internalizes self-care as an expression of self-respect and self-love. Parents model emotional health when they validate each other and teach the child how to communicate painful feelings naturally—crying when sad and talking out anger rather than acting it out. The parents consistently model healthy behavior in their actions. When the child is ready, sexuality is explained in an age-appropriate context.

These parents do not attempt to rescue their children every time a mistake is made. They allow the child to feel bad about wrong choices and figure out a way to correct their mistakes. When parents allow their children to experience the consequences of their choices, they are facilitating maturity and independence. Through trial and error, the youth develops the habit of making good decisions without parental interception or intrusion.

> **Parents model emotional health when they validate each other and teach the child how to communicate painful feelings naturally.**

As a teenager, a solid inner core has formed, and the youth is able to manage normal social anxiety without the need to go along with the crowd just to feel accepted. The parents explain that all kids feel nervous, and there's no need to drink or use drugs just to feel better or to try and fit in. They explain that it's okay to be a nonjudgmental observer without participating. The child is also encouraged to hang out with other kids who don't drink or use drugs. These kids are nervous too, but they can manage their social anxiety in a natural way, and they can enjoy time together without getting high.

As a strong sense of self and identity develops, the adolescent begins to form an idea of a future life and career. The child's desires are explored and honored, while the parents provide guidance without imposing their own secret wishes and desires on the child.

This individual grows into a secure adult who feels that the world and the people in it are safe. This individual can take life's disappointments, mourn them, learn and grow from them, and move on. Goals are not aborted because of temporary failure, and those setbacks are used to learn and to be better. The young adult learns to navigate their way through life, making the best of it.

While this description might seem otherworldly to many, psycho-analysts, starting with Freud, have known the importance of a well-developed ego and the ability to adapt to and cope with life's ups and downs. Countless studies have validated the importance of healthy childhood development. It does not mean, however, that a healthy childhood is a prerequisite for a fulfilling life, only that you might need to work harder at it if you lacked a solid foundation.

> **The child who feels cared for and loved will be governed by love rather than pain.**

You might be thinking that I'm living in some kind of la-la land and not seeing family life through a realistic lens. After all, with so many different cultures and socioeconomic classes, how can I possibly oversimplify such a complex issue? So let me be clear: I'm not saying that any childhood has to be (or even should be) perfect, as confronting difficulties is also an important part of becoming a strong and capable adult. But a childhood that is safe enough and fulfilling enough to allow the child to enjoy life without having to engage in artificial "okay-ness" creates a strong foundation for developing a fulfilling life in adulthood. Bottom line: a child has to be provided enough emotional security and empathic involvement, either by a parent or a respected role model, to grow up with the awareness that they are whole and unbroken. The child who feels cared for and loved will be governed by love rather than fear. A child is inspired to do better rather than motivated with pain. Children who grow up in an abusive or neglectful environment most likely will struggle with some manifestation of addiction at some point in their lives—either by being addicted, being attracted to someone who has an addiction, or both.

After reading the above, perhaps you can identify some things that were missing in your childhood and learn how to better care for yourself now. Many people don't have a clue what it means to love. For starters, you can reread this section and pinpoint specific acts of love that were missing in your childhood. Then you can start to correct those inadequacies with acts of self-love. You are now the adult who meets your own needs in healthy ways, which includes allowing others to help you when necessary.

Good Enough, Not Perfect

There is no perfect way to raise a child, and when parents are expecting a child, they are not given a how-to manual for rearing children. In spite of many imperfections in how a child is raised, children turn out fine. Minor errors are overlooked, and if the big errors are acknowledged and healed, they, too, are left in the past. However, if traumatic moments are not acknowledged and addressed, they fester into a wound that forms the invisible hole that drives addiction.

Let's start off by saying that most caretakers do not intend to harm. Parenting strategies tend to be handed down from one generation to the next. These inherited values and behaviors can set in place all sorts of dysfunctional patterns and beliefs. Worse, children raised in families that are suffering from addiction, mental health problems, and other dysfunctions have the compounded challenge of being at the mercy of people who are too ill to know what they are doing. Children brought up in these environments often find themselves as adults following in the footsteps of the very people they vowed never to emulate. If you are willing to examine what has happened in your family tree, you can be the one to stop the dysfunction for future generations.

Early Trauma and Later Addiction

We now know that abuse can start before a child is even born. A mother who is abusing drugs or alcohol while pregnant, or not taking care of herself in other ways, is exposing her unborn child to the potential risk of permanent damage. For example, a pregnant woman who abuses substances could give birth to a child who suffers from fetal alcohol syndrome or drug dependence, conditions that could affect the baby's neurological and physical well-being for life. If she isn't eating properly or if she's smoking, the developing fetus will be more susceptible to low birth weight, which can increase the risk of psychiatric problems later in life.[2]

Excessive stress during the pregnancy (such as combative relationships, financial hardship, excessive work schedule), causes the release of stress hormones, such as adrenaline and cortisol, in the mother's body. Excessive amounts of these hormones could result in the child developing mood disorders later.[3]

From the moment of birth, we begin to form our concept of ourselves and our place in the world. When nurtured and taught love and respect for themselves and others, most children will grow up to become well-adjusted and happy adults. When children learn to share and receive love, they will naturally balance the needs of self and others.

Child-rearing errors produce a different result. If a child is abused, neglected, or raised in a home that does not feel safe, that child develops an image of an unsafe world. These children perceive relationships as painful and lacking love, or they grow to believe that life is cruel and a place of lack. Placed in survival mode, these children grow up feeling a void inside, an invisible hole that they can't seem to fill no matter what. They are left with an insatiable need, and they usually have no idea why or what the source is. Many people go their entire lives feeling the invisible hole and trying to fill it with addictive behaviors without understanding that their behavior is trying to replace the love and nurturing that was lacking in their childhood.

There is a difference between abuse and trauma. All abuse is traumatic, but not all trauma is abuse. Trauma can result from the death of a loved one, an illness that causes a child to miss school and friends, loss of a favorite pet or love object, or any other type of painful event. If a child suffers loss, it is traumatic but not abusive, unless the child is not allowed the opportunity to grieve.

Sometimes a parent will tell a child that it's not okay to feel sad when a loss has occurred, or they encourage the child to hide or suppress feelings in some other way. The only appropriate reaction to a child's pain is to show empathy, provide comfort, and create an opening for the child to talk about the experience, so the pain is released and moved beyond. If that pain remains unaddressed, it turns into suffering and unresolved grief.

An addictive personality develops from unhealed trauma that lodges in the psyche as a wound.

I will not cover every form of abuse that children endure, but if you experienced a deep pain or frightening experience when you were a child and that wound has not been addressed and healed, consider yourself someone who has carried trauma your whole life.

I'd like to stress that it is not my intention to blame anyone—that is a rabbit hole with no end. We tend to parent in the same way we were parented and simply don't know any better. To heal, we do have to understand what happened, and until we face that truth, we cannot face the feelings that keep the hole intact.

> **An addictive personality develops from unhealed trauma that lodges in the psyche as a wound.**

Children are subjected to different types of abuse: emotional, physical, sexual, and verbal, as well as neglect. Each of these can occur in varying degrees of intensity and duration, and each can be blatant or subtle. They all deepen the sense of emptiness and craving—the invisible hole—which lures people into the addiction maze.

Emotional abuse occurs when a child's mind is exposed to cruelty in the form of unfair or inappropriate encounters. For example, a child is deeply saddened or scared or both when witnessing their caretakers engaging in violent or excessively loud arguments. Children often come out of these situations feeling that they are responsible for the conflict, separation, or divorce. This can be compounded when one of the parents is alienated (intentionally or unintentionally) from the child. This form of abandonment puts full responsibility on one parent and deprives the child of a vital relationship.

Another form of emotional abuse is when children are expected to perform tasks and responsibilities beyond their maturity level. No one should expect five-year-olds to cook their own meals or be responsible for major housekeeping, yet this is a frequent occurrence in some households. Parents are supposed to be there for their children, not the other way around.

Emotional blackmail happens when a parent tells a child to help them keep a secret or hide a wrongful act. Children aren't impressed when a parent flaunts an affair, and they become torn when they witness this type of betrayal. Quite a few patients have reported painful and confusing memories of witnessing a parent with a lover. The same holds true when a parent unexpectedly dies and is replaced too soon with a surrogate. One teenaged patient, sobbing during a session told his father, "Mom just died a few months ago and I don't feel right about being around your girlfriend. I don't like seeing her in the kitchen, I don't like her in mom's bed, I don't want her to pick me up from school." His father, filled with his own grief, had never considered his son's feelings. Fortunately, the boy was given an opportunity to find his voice. When they were able to discuss the matter openly, new boundaries were established, and eventually, the girlfriend became a welcome part of the family.

Young children haven't yet learned how to justify unhealthy behavior, so when they are forced to witness it and go along with it, it is confusing and painful. When the pain is held in and never validated, it begins to drill a psychological hole in the child's self-esteem.

Children are emotionally abused when told that their birth was the result of an unplanned pregnancy and is a hardship on the family, instilling a feeling of being an unwanted burden. Children who are favored over their siblings by one or both parents feel guilty, and those who are seen as lesser than their sibling(s) feel angry. Either way, blatant favoritism is emotionally abusive.

It is emotionally abusive for a parent to make promises without keeping them, then make the child feel guilty for feeling disappointed. Without providing an adequate reason or simply blowing off any explanation, the parent teaches the child that it's unsafe to trust, and it's wrong to feel disappointed. In either case, raising a child's expectations without delivering and not owning up to the failure to follow through are abusive.

I've heard this typical scenario countless times: A young child waits for a drunk parent to come home, and upon return, the overly cheerful (guilt-ridden) parent apologizes for missing dinner but promises to take the child to buy a new bicycle (or other toy) the following morning. When the parent still hasn't arisen by noon, the frustrated child attempts to awaken the parent, only to be yelled at for the disturbance. As two o'clock rolls around and the parent emerges, the child regains excitement about the new bicycle, but instead of going to the store, they are forced to accompany the parent to the liquor store. When the disappointed child cries and asks about the bicycle, the parent yells at the child for being selfish. This youngster learns not only to distrust but also to expect disappointment from a person who is supposed to be trustworthy and whom they had counted on.

> **Parents are supposed to be there for their children,
> not the other way around.**

Denying what a child accurately sees, hears, or senses and lying to a child so as to invalidate a child's perception of reality are abuse. When children are micromanaged and trained to act like robots or overloaded with rules and regulations, their sense of freedom, independence, and spontaneity is squelched. When a child witnesses a parent who becomes intoxicated, steals, or otherwise breaks the law, the child is witnessing a parent who is out of control, thus creating fear and a sense of instability.

Emotional abuse may happen outside of the core family, with other relatives, or within schools or religious institutions. Anyone whose behavior causes a child to feel less than, shameful, or afraid is facilitating abuse rather than inspiring good choices. An angry scowl or dismissive attitude can lower a child's self-concept as much as harsh words. When children are told they are stupid, failures, sinful, or otherwise unacceptable, these messages will penetrate the child's ego and fester as a persistent sense of unworthiness. Withholding love, retaliating, and humiliating children in public are other ways children are made to feel worthless.

Neglect occurs when a child's basic needs for food, shelter, physical safety, and love are not properly met. When funds are available, no child should go hungry or without the nourishment that supports strong physical growth and development. A child should be adequately clothed, sheltered, and raised in a safe and sanitary environment, so that home provides a feeling of physical comfort and safety. Anything less than this is a form of neglect.

Even parents who live in poverty manage to raise children whose basic needs are met—perhaps they wear clothing that has been donated and eat low-cost foods—but if they still are shown love and concern, these children can grow up to thrive. I have worked with people who knew they had less than their schoolmates but who felt they received adequate care because a parent made their clothes, cooked delicious but inexpensive meals, and knew how to make a dollar last. I recently read a book about Jackie Robinson and how his mother managed to provide five children with their basic needs without the assistance of welfare.[4] The devotion this mother had for meeting the needs of her children produced a son who is recognized as one of the greatest and most respected men of all time. There are countless parents who mustered all they could to make sure their children survived in challenging situations. These children grew up to know they were loved even if there was a lack of material things.

Parents who are good producers can provide material things for their child but often neglect to spend adequate time with them, compromising the child's mental health. In a study by Jeff Greenhaus and Steward Friedman involving about nine hundred professional parents, they found that "children's emotional health was higher when parents believed that family should come first, regardless of the amount of time they spent working."[5] Children raised in families who have an abundance of everything but time often feel lonely and unloved. When adults don't have time to talk with their children, do things with them, and be there to support them emotionally, the children will feel less important than their parents' preoccupations. The point I am making here is that when it comes to raising emotionally and physically healthy children, love goes a lot further than money.

Children suffer neglect when they are not provided training for basic life skills or are denied medical care for good health, especially when that care is readily available. When parents place children in roles that are beyond their understanding, such as caring for much younger children, maintaining the home, and cooking for themselves, they have neglected to care for their children.

Feelings of abandonment occur when a child is left alone for unreasonable periods of time, is forgotten about, or is left to be cared for by others rather than by the parents (without reason or explanation). When a child is not held, cuddled, played with, or paid attention to often enough, they are left to feel unimportant and unworthy of attention or love—this is emotional abandonment.

There are several scenarios where children are subject to sexual abuse. It is never appropriate for an adult to make a romantic gesture toward a child or ever initiate any type of sexual touch. Sexual abuse could occur with an acquaintance, parent, relative, mentor, sibling, teacher, or anyone who comes into contact with the child, including total strangers. Sexual abuse can range from inappropriate comments to rape and everything in between. It can happen at any age. I've worked with emergency medical staff who've talked about babies who've been sexually assaulted and even raped.

Parents who attempt to have sexual relations with a child are deeply disturbed and most likely are reenacting their own childhood trauma. It's also inappropriate for children to be witness to sexual movies or inappropriate sexual behavior from adults. When a child is exposed to these types of situations and not properly supervised, they are likely to experiment with siblings and peers. It is normal for kids to be curious about one another, and a certain amount of exploration is natural. It has been alarming to hear numerous stories of kids who were not properly supervised and at early ages had sex with brothers, sisters, and friends, and those experiences forever haunted them.

Some adults are covertly sexually abusive toward their children. Parents who flirt with their children, act seductively, parade around half-dressed, or are overly touchy-feely are taking the risk of being eroticized by their child. When parents discuss their sex lives with their children, they are crossing an unhealthy line of fantasy that their child is an adult. Children need to perceive their parents as wholesome adults, not sex objects.

Emotional incest occurs when a parent uses a child as a surrogate partner. The child is used as a confidant, a support person, or a substitute for the absentee parent. Expected to fill every role but having sex with the parent, the child is placed in the adult role of caretaker or partner, which creates an emotional bind where the child feels both powerful and trapped: empowered by a sense of superiority and simultaneously robbed of freedom. Adults need to share their personal lives, social interests, and adult concerns with other adults, not their kids.

Verbal abuse causes a child to feel humiliated and worthless. Name-calling and raging at a child are not only belittling, but they also teach a child to yell rather than talk out angry feelings. Talking down to, using sarcasm, or criticizing a child also diminishes self-esteem. All verbal abuse is a noncreative way to communicate frustration. To use fear to enforce compliance destroys a child's desire to make good choices for the sake of feeling good.

Physical abuse can be moderate to severe and is never an acceptable method of punishment, regardless of the child's mistakes. When a child misbehaves, administering a time-out, temporary loss of a privilege, or loss of a favored object will teach the child logical consequences from bad choices. Physical abuse occurs when a parent is too angry or too unskilled to know any different and administers force. When children are struck by their parents or hit with objects to the point of bodily harm, a permanent mark is left on the child's self-image. Children who are yanked can suffer dislocated shoulders. Children who are thrown can have broken bones. Children who are shaken often suffer brain damage. According to the National Center for Fatality Review and Prevention, head and skeletal trauma, internal bleeding from kicks to the abdomen, and burning are the major causes of physical injuries related to child abuse.[6]

> All verbal abuse is a noncreative way to
> communicate frustration.

Let us remember that the invisible hole has many opportunities to form from experiences outside of the home and by someone else who hurts the child. In many cases of sexual abuse, the perpetrator threatens to harm the child or another family member if the child reports it. Sometimes the abuse is reported and the parents fail to address the issue because of their own inadequacies. Regardless of the circumstances, if the wound is not healed, it does not vanish; it remains hidden in the unconscious. These are just some types of abuse that create the invisible hole.

Sometimes a patient will tell me, "It wasn't that bad, we had everything we needed, and at least I wasn't beaten or raped. Yea, my dad yelled at me and told me I was a loser, and my mom ignored it, but so what?" My stance on this is that regardless of the method of abuse and where it falls on any spectrum, if you suffered trauma, you suffered trauma; your experiences don't need to be compared to anyone else's. Anything that causes a child to feel like less than a lovable human being will open up the invisible hole.

Children who feel loved and cared for and are raised to trust their own perceptions and instincts transfer those experiences to the world outside and can cope with the imperfections of life. Children need to be disciplined to learn boundaries and respect for themselves and others. However, discipline should never inflict lasting physical or emotional harm. In my opinion, it is far better to allow a child to face the consequences—loss of a toy or planned event—than to use physical force or emotional torture. The former may be harder on everyone involved because it requires more parental effort. But enforcing consequences, even if it inconveniences others, leaves more of a healthy lasting impression than spanking or long-term, unreasonable restrictions that result in resentment.

No parent is perfect; I've made some of the worst mistakes. If you are a parent, it won't do any good to feel guilty. Children are resilient and can endure imperfect parenting. If a parenting mistake is acknowledged and corrected, children are quick to forgive, but if the parent fails to acknowledge, continues, or justifies inappropriate behavior, the wound will fester. Most of us make the same errors as our parents did, or we make new errors by overcompensating in an attempt to do the opposite. The goal is to keep on learning and improving. If we can do even a little bit better than our parents, each generation will do a better job at producing healthier children, free from the bondage of addiction.

Self-Evaluation Questionnaire

Identify Healthy Styles of Parenting

1. Make a list with two columns. On one side, list the components of a healthy child-rearing template, including your own ideas. Circle the ones you received as a child. Next, make a list of all the components that were missing in your childhood. Underline the ones you are willing to provide for yourself now.

2. Do you feel you were micromanaged as a child? How did this affect you?

3. Were you neglected? Hungry, cold, lonely, lost? If so, describe what caused you to feel this way.

4. Were you emotionally abused? If so, how?

5. Physically abused? If so, how?

6. Sexually abused? If so, how?

7. What do you think caused your parents to raise you the way they did?

8. If you are a parent, what parenting patterns did you repeat (or are you repeating) with your children?

9. If you are a parent, how would you like to do (or have done) things differently?

7

THE PAIN TEMPLATE

The wound is the place where the Light enters you.

—Rumi

Addiction is like touching a hot burner over and over. You don't think you will get burned the next time, but you do. The important question to ask is, why keep touching the burner?

Becoming aware that you have been trying to fill an invisible hole is not enough to stay clear of or beat addiction. There's some work to be done first. You must come to understand how your brain has been wired with a specific template and how that template has kept you going up and down and all around the maze. Then you can start creating a new template for your future.

During early childhood, the unconscious mind operates like a computer and records everything it sees and hears. The recording forms a mental template that is permanently branded in the mind. That template can be one of painful or pleasurable memories, or a combination of both.

This template becomes a point of reference for adult life. It resembles the concept of the Imago that Harville Hendrix describes in his classic *Getting the Love You Want*. The difference is that his model focuses solely on uncovering the source of frustrations within a romantic relationship. I use the term "pain template" because I have seen in my decades-long practice that people create all kinds of relationships destined to retrigger childhood wounds from various sources.

Children who witness loving parents, who have their needs met, and who grow up feeling safe develop a pleasure template. Children who witness or experience abuse develop a pain template. People who were harmed as children are likely to continue to be harmed (victims) or will turn around and harm others (perpetrators) because that is their mental map for child-rearing and interpersonal relationships—it's how they were programmed.

Most people know that it is never good to be abused or be abusive, and yet many people reenact their childhood nightmares even after they have sworn they never would. The internal template veers in the same direction, and it's impossible to change without the tools. As long as the pain template is reenacted, the wound grows and all nontherapeutic attempts to get rid of the pain only make the hole bigger. It is a vicious cycle.

> **Children who witness or experience abuse develop a pain template.**

Freud explains that when we are triggered by someone (positively or negatively), we are experiencing transference. Here's how transference works: if your mother was hypercritical of you when you were a child, that transfers to your experience now as an adult, so every time you perceive (accurately or not) someone being critical of you, you have a strong reaction, sometimes to the point of obsessing about it for days. I'm not talking about mild annoyances that might trigger a minor reaction that evaporates like a wisp of cloud. I'm talking about a tornado that has been brewing for years—the vortex around the invisible hole. The current event has a root from an earlier wound that gets triggered and causes you to feel flooded with emotion. I call it "going nuclear," when you feel an extreme reaction that you can't shake off. Two common, ineffective strategies people use to push out their intense reactions are to blame someone else (projection) for the discomfort or kill it off through self-medicating. Either one of these strategies represents a missed opportunity to heal a wound you might have carried your entire life.

It doesn't matter which current event is triggering the reaction; if you're going nuclear, it's about the past. The event has triggered some childhood abuse or trauma and detonates the reaction. Here's an example: if your parents often kept you waiting during your childhood, you may have stood outside of the school, all by yourself, waiting and waiting, feeling more and more afraid. Now that you're an adult, when someone is late, you relive that fear, and you're not even aware of why you feel so upset. By the time the person does arrive, you are so charged, you lash out or hold on to the negative energy generated by your reaction, and your friend has no idea why you are so upset by a five- or ten-minute delay. You're triggered because in those moments of waiting, you are reliving your five-year-old terror of waiting on a street corner, near dark, all alone and wondering if anyone would ever arrive.

Every patient with whom I have ever worked demonstrated the pattern of reenacting the pain template, then attempting to medicate away the pain. Let's take Karl, who was born into a family with two teenage parents. His was an unplanned birth. He felt his parents loved each other, but his wound started to form when weekends were frequently ruined because his parents got drunk and fought. By the time he was ten, his parents had divorced; his mother was only twenty-three, his father twenty-four. That wound formed a deeper hole when he was shuffled around to different relatives. He felt angry, confused, and abandoned. He missed having his family together, and the pain of loss and loneliness widened the invisible hole inside.

In his early teens, Karl started trying to fill his invisible hole with drugs, and he stole to support his new habit. At age sixteen, after stealing from an employer, he was arrested but was able to work out a plea and avoid going to jail. Karl continued to use drugs, and his life revolved around partying and his new drug of choice—sex.

At age seventeen, Karl dropped out of high school to work full-time in construction. His dependence on drugs increased, and he continued to have run-ins with the law. When he was twenty-one, at a friend's party, a young girl approached him for sex; she was fourteen (the same age as Karl's mother when he was born), and he complied. Several days later, he was arrested for having sex with a minor and was convicted. His own mother being a teenager when he was born, combined with his developmental arrest as a teen, distorted his thinking. "I now realize it was stupid of me. We'd been drinking and I didn't know her age when she came into my bedroom naked. I deserved to go to jail but didn't understand it at the time," he told me. He spent two years in jail without fully comprehending what he'd done wrong. Over the next decade after his release, he was in and out of jail on convictions of disorderly conduct and drug-related charges. During his final incarceration, he was introduced to a 12-Step program and stopped using alcohol and drugs. This was the first time he'd turned his life in a positive direction. Once sober, Karl stopped getting into trouble with the law. He began therapy because he wanted to get married, but he and his girlfriend often fought—mostly about sex.

Karl's pain template for relationships began when he witnessed his (teenaged) parents' intense fighting, followed by their divorce and the instability that ensued. The widening pain gnawed away at him, and the invisible hole that formed grew with each recurring painful event. Now that drugs and alcohol were no longer an option, he had become obsessed with using sex to medicate his wound. He wanted to have sex at least once a day, and his girlfriend felt overwhelmed by his demands.

> **You can heal your reactions and be comfortable in your own body.**

Karl had started using at a young age, which only buried his painful memories and delayed his ability to mature. Once Karl recognized that he had been using drugs and sex to avoid feeling unresolved childhood pain, he had a decision to make. To break free of addiction, he would have to face the pain his addiction was covering up, heal the wound, and then learn a new template for healthy, intimate relationships, with sex being only one component. When I last met with Karl, he said he would be back in touch when he was ready to do the work. He has touched base from time to time, but he has yet to be willing to commit.

Once you are able to recognize that you can heal your reactions and be comfortable in your own body, you won't need to escape your feelings anymore. By following the steps in this book, you can learn to embrace your emotions so you won't need to self-medicate. When you perceive these same emotions as a valued aid rather than your enemy, you can give yourself the power to steer away from the addictive nosedive and stay on the course to freedom.

Candy-Coated Pain

The pain template isn't always a result of an obvious trauma. Some forms of pain are inflicted in the name of love. Children who are smothered with food or care suffer this type of pain. It is important that children be allowed to experience their feelings and be taught how to release them in healthy ways. If children are sad and encouraged to cry, they will find an emotional release in expelling the pain. When angry children are taught to talk about the anger, they will not act out in destructive ways. Some parents don't like to see their children suffer, and they inadvertently offer the kind of help that teaches suppression, such as telling their children they should "buck up" or "don't cry; you're fine."

Joanna started therapy because she was depressed. When I first met her, her strawberry-blond hair was unruly, she was so heavy she had difficulty walking, and she seemed emotionally shut down. She had a twenty-year-old daughter, Lisa, whom she had raised alone. Joanna's life revolved around her medical career and food. She had been in treatment for an eating disorder and had lost weight, but she relapsed when her daughter attempted suicide.

Lisa had taken a drug overdose after she remembered being sexually assaulted by her babysitter when she was only two years old. Joanna admitted that it was true, and she was overwhelmed with guilt that she had allowed a man she barely knew to care for her child.

Joanna also had been raised by a single mom. She remembered her mother as a cold woman who only showed love through food. Whenever Joanna was sad, her mother told her, "Here, eat this; you will feel better." Food was the suggested solution for any problem. By the time Joanna entered first grade, she was so overweight the other kids made fun of her, further expanding her wound.

Her invisible hole had begun to form, and she filled this void with the only thing she knew—more food. When Joanna entered high school, her life centered on eating and making good grades. When she was finishing nursing school and interning at the hospital, Joanna was so lonely and depressed that she was easily seduced when a guy she worked with showed an interest in her. Their first date ended in her first sexual experience, nonconsensual, and that was the last she heard from him.

Filled with feelings of abandonment and regret, Joanna consoled herself the way she always had: with food. At first, she thought her weight gain was related to bingeing on pastries and candy, but after several months of missed periods, she discovered she was pregnant. Twenty years later and a hundred pounds heavier, the crisis with her daughter's attempted suicide propelled her to get help.

Even though Joanna's eating disorder had been treated, the invisible hole remained intact, and she continued to reenact the pain template her mother taught her: suppress the pain that caused the wound, then fill the invisible hole with food. As Joanna progressed through therapy, she regularly attended a 12-Step meeting for food addicts, and instead of eating sugar and wheat, she was able to access and release emotions bottled inside of her. She also engaged in family therapy, so Lisa could talk about her sexual abuse and Joanna could offer her daughter the maternal support needed to heal her painful trauma.

When Pain Templates Collide

The most intriguing aspect of pain templates is how two people tend to meet and match their pain templates in such a way that perfectly reenacts both people's past wounds. We most often hear how this plays out in romantic relationships, but the pain template collision can occur in any type of relationship—parent to child, friend to friend, peer to peer. These relationships offer a golden opportunity to heal the past and start anew. First, however, you have to be aware that all your reactions are about the past, and when triggered, you have to use those feelings to heal the past. More about this later.

> **Pain template collision can occur in any type of relationship.**

The most common setup for a pain template collision is when the child of an addict is unconsciously drawn into a relationship with an addict. Addicts try to fill the invisible hole by using the other person as a human repair kit; at the same time, children of addicts are trying to fill their invisible hole by repairing the addict, so they can finally receive the love and attention they did not get as a child. Both are trying to find their way out of the maze, but they are merely reenacting the same pain templates that were created in their childhoods. These attempts to fill the invisible hole by reenacting the childhood nightmare will fail unless both people in the relationship commit to doing the work that will heal the wounds that drive them.

There will never be enough of anything external to fill the invisible hole. You can have all the booze, drugs, food, power, sex, attention, and anything else you want, but all of those things are like pouring poison into your soul. If you want to get well, you will have to stop hurting yourself and learn how to fill the invisible hole with actions that will heal the wound. You can stop using and go to the best therapists and treatment centers, but that won't be enough if you don't address the invisible hole. The following questions will help you identify if you have a pain template and if so, how it was formed.

Self-Evaluation Questionnaire

Identify Your Pain Template

1. What type of relationship did you witness from your parents (loving, warm, affectionate, cold, violent, a mixture)?
2. Did you feel you were wanted as a child?
3. What early painful events started forming the hole? What was the most painful?
4. List any negative messages you were told that made you feel less than.
5. How have those negative messages continued throughout your life?
6. How did you cope with painful feelings?
7. Were you forced to think or feel a certain way or were you ostracized (at home, school, a religious institution, or elsewhere)?
8. Did you ever feel you were physically hurt by a loved one (other than by accident)? What happened?
9. Was there enough to eat and enough personal care in your family? If not, what was missing?
10. Did you spend endless hours alone? Were you lonely? Did you feel that you weren't important to your parents at times? If the answer to any of these is yes, write down which memories these questions bring to light.

11. Did anyone ever try to touch you in a way that felt sexually inappropriate or wrong to you? If so, what did you do?
12. Did you feel comfortable with the way your parents dressed at home (or were not dressed)? Clarify what you saw and what you felt.
13. Did anything else happen in your childhood that you have had a hard time living with? If so, describe the experience now if you can.

8

ROMANTIC IMPRINTS

I'm not crying because of you; you're not worth it.
I'm crying because my delusion of who you were was shattered
by the truth of who you are.

—**Steve Maraboli**, *Unapologetically You*

Pain templates can be played out in any kind of relationship, but romantic relationships deserve a chapter all their own because they can be so intense. We also have the added complication of the euphoria and addictive brain chemistry that gets activated through romantic attraction and sex. Often the most intense romantic relationships begin based solely on physical attraction and quickly devolve when the hormone high starts to wear off. When there's a breakup, the sober addict is ill-equipped to cope with the intensity of withdrawal emotions and is likely to relapse. I have seen more people relapse on substances after a relationship went south than any other trigger.

The common cause for an immediate magnetic attraction is the romantic imprint. An imprint is a sensory-visual image that is branded into the mind. A romantic imprint occurs when the first blush of passion overtakes you, usually around the fifth or sixth grade. Suddenly, someone stirs you in such a way that you are never the same. Your heart goes pitter-patter, and you feel flushed, excited, as if you can walk on air. Everyone else pales in this person's presence. You can't stop thinking about them, you have sleepless nights, and you may even lose your appetite. You find a part of you that has never emerged before, one full of creativity, excitement, and longing.

When I tell people they have such an imprint, they often rebuff the idea, but I invite you to let this idea marinate a little bit and see what awareness might surface. Without fail, every person who has given this notion some thought has been able to retrieve the image of that first person, whose appearance became the preferred look of any future potential partners.

We all know that first blush of puppy love is healthy and normal, but when a young person is carrying unhealed trauma that has created an invisible hole, the first romantic imprint can be addictive. An image of who you saw in that moment becomes stamped in the mind and, once linked to that first, innocent puppy-love feeling, can turn into a drug-like driving force to seek that same high.

Addicted to Love

Though few ever recognize it, ever since that first crush, we have a natural tendency to be attracted to the same physical type as our imprint. A healthy, well-adapted person who is not prone to addiction is able to discern that physical attraction doesn't necessarily equate to compatibility, so they will weigh physical attraction as well as other elements of compatibility in considering a potential partner. On the other hand, a person carrying an unhealed wound and who is vulnerable to addiction is way more likely to mistake the effects of a powerful physical attraction for true love.

Laura and Mike came to therapy because they wanted to stop fighting. She was tall and thin, with long black hair and green eyes; he was also tall, with brown hair and eyes. They were both in their midforties and physically fit. Laura had been practicing law for several years; Mike was a manager at a local Cadillac dealer. Neither had been married or had children.

They had met at a 12-Step social function, and from the moment they set eyes on each other, it was as though no one else was in the room. They were inseparable the whole evening. After leaving the meeting, they went for coffee, then back to Mike's place for "wild sex." Two weeks later, Mike told Laura she was "the one" he'd been waiting for and asked her to move in with him.

This is a classic beginning of an unconscious relationship driven by a strong mutual imprint match. Things went well for the first three months, then the fighting began when they triggered each other's pain templates. Laura said Mike was moody, and Mike said Laura was a workaholic. A pattern ensued where neither attempted to understand the other, the bickering intensified to screaming, and Laura would leave the house. After several days, Mike would become heartsick and text Laura to come back. They would reunite and have blissful sex. But after a few days, the pattern would start all over again.

Having worked with many people in addictive relationships, I understood how their pain templates had collided and how hard it was for them to break their patterns. Like many couples I've seen, by the time they came to therapy, Laura and Mike were emotionally drained. Mike would blame Laura for not paying enough attention to him, and Laura would call Mike a control freak. All of the empathy exercises and active listening techniques I tried to teach ended in fights where words were thrown like punches.

> A person carrying an unhealed wound and who is vulnerable to addiction is way more likely to mistake the effects of a powerful physical attraction for true love.

"You didn't do your homework; you obviously don't care about me," Mike would tell Laura, and she would reply, "You're crazy. I can't do this anymore!" All of their energy went into blaming one another, leaving them with no energy for compassion or building understanding. It was clear to me that Mike and Laura had been pulled into each other's imprint, but without a foundation of trust built over time, their sexual attraction for each other was not enough for a sustainable relationship. On top of that, each had personality traits that activated the other's childhood wounds.

When their wounds collided, their pain templates were reenacted, preventing them from being present in the here and now. Unless and until they each healed the wounds that had triggered them, they would not learn how to healthily share their pain and show empathy for the other person. Even more important, they would continue to miss the opportunity to recognize that the wounds they triggered in each other could be a door to healing the past, if they were willing to open it. As long as they believed they were reacting to their partner, and not their past, their chance for change and growth was nil.

Laura's mother was prone to rage. She always had found fault with Laura. The oldest of five children, Laura was forced to take responsibility for her siblings and couldn't remember "just being a kid." Her sense of responsibility for her family put her in the role of a surrogate mother rather than a child. Her parents were never married, her father was absent throughout her childhood, and she never formed a relationship with him.

Mike, too, had a father who had abandoned the family when Mike was young; he was raised by his mother with whom he "never felt safe." He remembers all through his childhood feeling manipulated through guilt. He felt like he was supposed to take care of his mother, not the reverse. He could not recall her ever paying much attention to him; it was all about her. At the car dealership, Mike was required to work long hours, and when he came home, he wanted Laura to pay attention to him. Laura's job as an attorney was stressful, and when she came home, she wanted to relax for the evening and take some time for herself. Her lack of interest in Mike set off his pain template of having had a mother who used him for her own needs, and he relived the painful wound of abandonment. When Mike would become angry with Laura, it triggered her pain template of her mother raging at her when she didn't jump up to tend to the kids.

Neither Mike nor Laura had parents who modeled healthy parenting or a healthy adult partnership. They both had assumed the position of adult replacements for the missing parent. When triggered by each other in their relationship, they were consumed by old feelings of not being properly cared for, followed by anger and resentment. The unconscious reenactment of their dysfunctional childhood families only wore them down because they were psychologically living in the past rather than being able to enjoy each other in the now.

No amount of therapy could help this couple until they were each willing to recognize that they were reenacting the pain templates of their childhoods: Laura's resentment of her mother's demands on her and Mike's feelings about a mother who'd emotionally abandoned him and used him to fill her own needs. Both agreed to do the work necessary to heal their individual wounds and learn how to communicate in an entirely new way. In spite of threatening to leave therapy whenever they felt uncomfortable, they managed to stick it out and keep their appointments.

Slowly, Laura and Mike began to see that they each were reacting to an unhealed past. They both worked through their old pain, but as the emotional intensity lessened, boredom set in. Mike and Laura had known only the wanton electricity of their sexual relationship, and now they had to build the circuitry of friendship and trust.

At one point, Laura made the choice to move out and continue to see Mike in couple's therapy. She realized she had never lived alone, and she wanted to learn how. At first Mike threatened to break up with her, but Laura communicated that she did not want to break up; she wanted to build something new.

She followed through by spending time with Mike and insisting they do more activities like going out for coffee or walks, so they could talk. As they got to know one another, they began to understand that their attraction had been primarily physical, and they were not compatible. They had little in common, and the relationship slowly dissipated. When Laura's firm relocated her to an office in another state, she stopped therapy, and eventually the couple parted on good terms.

Even though their relationship did not last, it was not a failure. Unlike many couples, Laura and Mike had the courage to face the internal pain the relationship had brought up, and instead of blaming, they each were able to heal. Having addressed their pain templates, they are more likely to make progressive improvement in their relationship choices in the future.

My husband, Skip, and I are an example of unmatched imprints who have successfully navigated our way into an intimate relationship. He was my imprint; I was not his. Even so, we started off as friends, and over many months, our relationship blossomed into romance as our respect and enjoyment of each other grew. Though we each came into the relationship with our individual pain templates, we had healed our wounds enough to have ventured out of the maze, and we were able to use our conflicts as a doorway to deeper growth. In our relationship, we both are able to be vulnerable, share our pasts, and gain an understanding of each other's triggers. This understanding enables us to use those triggers as an opportunity to heal another piece of the past rather than reenact old wounds. For example, I've told him, "I feel anxious when you're late and don't tell me because when I was little, I was often waiting for hours for someone to wake up and take care of me." He might tell me, "When you tell me how to do things, it reminds me of my mother's incessant control of my life." This way of communicating allows us to view each other's actions and reactions without taking them personally and to be more sensitive and aware of how we trigger each other. Through this ongoing practice, we have built a relationship that allows us to feel close, safe, and cared for.

The Addiction of Codependency

Another manifestation of addiction is known as codependency. Instead of a person being addicted to a thing or a behavior, codependency represents an addiction to another person. Sometimes a child whose parents were addicted grows up to be addicted to unhealthy people. Signs of codependency occur when one person's life revolves around another's, and all of the symptoms of addiction manifest, such as loss of control, attempt to control, needing more to get the same effect, negative consequences, loss of friends, loss of self-care, ill health, and symptoms of emotional and physical withdrawal in the face of losing the codependent connection. Codependency frequently happens with romantic couples, but it also occurs in many nonromantic relationships.

For example, parents who are codependent with their children either live vicariously through their children's success, or they take care of the child beyond a reasonable age of adulthood. Caretakers who live for another and lack a satisfying life of their own often are addicted to the person they care for, or in some cases, they are addicted to an organization or institution. Regardless of circumstance, when the codependent feels abandoned by the person (or organization) on whom they have placed their focus, the codependent will experience many if not all of the withdrawal symptoms of any other addiction.

A case in point: Melissa was referred to me by another therapist who told her she needed to grieve the loss of her son, Jess. Her world revolved around Jess as she unsuccessfully tried to control his drug habit. Melissa did not realize that all the fear-based things she did were not helping Jess. He started using drugs in high school and later dropped out, at which point he spent most of his time either hanging out with his drug-using friends or isolated in his room. Melissa's life was consumed with transporting him, cooking for him, and trying to meet his every need, all in the hope that he would change. She was not consciously aware that she was using her son as a substitute for a relationship with another adult.

> Instead of a person being addicted to a thing or a behavior, codependency represents an addiction to another person.

After his first overdose, Jess completed a thirty-day treatment program, then returned home. In spite of his therapist's urging, Melissa did not participate in his treatment and did not attend Al-Anon meetings because she felt "uncomfortable." Fearful her son would not get well without her, Melissa continued to manage his life, cooking and cleaning for him and supporting him financially. Jess did not attend recovery meetings, and with no sober friends or tools, he resumed his drug habit shortly after he came home. Tragically, a month after his return, Melissa found Jess unconscious in his bed. When the EMTs arrived, they were unable to resuscitate him, and he was pronounced dead at the scene.

When I asked her about her feelings, Melissa changed the subject and started talking about her sister, who it seemed Melissa was now taking care of. She complained that her sister was ordering her around and that she did not have any free time for herself. She'd switched her codependency addiction from her son to her sister.

When I pointed out that she must be traumatized, Melissa skipped over my inquiry and complained her sister was putting too much responsibility on her. I was struck by the fact that Melissa was unable to feel her suffering and functioned as if she were on autopilot. She told me her childhood had been awful but could not elaborate other than by stating that she never felt safe growing up. Any attempts to draw out her feelings were unsuccessful. Melissa canceled her second appointment, stating that her sister had told her they needed to help their parents and there wasn't enough money for therapy, which was the opposite of what she'd said initially: that she was ready to start investing in herself.

Melissa had set up her life to always rotate around another person's wants and needs, which, like any other manifestation of addiction, served as a distraction from her true feelings and responsibility for her own well-being. She thought she was helping others, but her actions didn't take into account the genuine needs of others or herself. Her caretaking had the secondary plus of keeping her emotionally preoccupied while attempting to cover up the invisible hole left by a lifetime of pain.

Many people think that therapy is some type of magical quick fix to a long-term problem. Even the best of therapists cannot help a patient who is unwilling to do the work. More often than not, patients use a therapist as a sounding board, but when it's time to go deeper and heal the wound, they opt out.

When I first meet with a patient, we agree to a treatment plan that includes frequency of visits as well as home assignments. I would say roughly two or three out of a hundred patients actually do the exercises. When it comes time to take a deeper look at the pain template so it can be healed, a great deal of resistance shows up.

> **Even the best of therapists cannot help a patient who is unwilling to do the work.**

Some work through it, but most don't. Addicts use their addiction to distract themselves from the feelings they have avoided their whole lives. Acting out the wound is dramatic, but it is also familiar. While it distracts from the real pain, it keeps the wound alive but not necessarily felt. Even though this is counterproductive to healing, the familiarity of being sucked into the drama provides temporary relief from facing the wound, which feels scary and uncomfortable.

Locked in Love

Sometimes we confuse love with pain. If you measure feelings of love by how much pain you're in, your brand of love is more about codependency than love. Every addiction represents an unhealed wound from your past, including codependent addiction to people or institutions. Ideally, your relationships form an interdependent connection based on supporting one another rather than on making demands for unmet childhood needs.

Codependency and love addiction are the two ways people reenact their original childhood wounds and substitute addiction to a person for genuine love. Unlike genuine love, codependency has a hidden agenda. *"What can you do for me, and what do I have to do to get that?"*

When you love yourself, you have no need to search for someone to take care of your needs or to complete you. You are able to decide whether or not to be together based on how good you are for one another and how well you complement each other's needs. When you share love with another, you wish for the other person everything you wish for yourself, including the freedom to leave. When people confuse pain with love, they often become addicted to the pain, mistaking it for love. To lose someone is painful and temporary; refusal to let go is ongoing torture.

Strangely enough, for the love addict, the pain seems preferable to the temporary void of a breakup. When a loss or the threat of a loss occurs, the pain that follows convinces an addict that love is causing that pain. Love, including self-love, has no pain because love knows no lack. It is complete unto itself and needs nothing. The addiction is ever-present to remind us of lack, and it tells us we must fear a loss because this love affair, friendship, or work connection will never be replaced. When we operate from such fear, we hang on to people long after they no longer need to be a part of our lives.

We must remember that all addictions are an expression of the same condition: an attempt to escape the feelings of emptiness and the vortex of pain around the invisible hole. Until an addicted person faces that pain and emptiness and heals it, life will be like a circus, where the addict takes the precarious swing from one trapeze to the next without a net.

Having read all this, if you see that you have been caught in the addiction maze, know that you do not have to stay in the maze any longer. There is a way out, and it's much quicker than you think. The question is: Are you willing to do what it takes to heal?

> **All addictions are an expression of the same condition: an attempt to escape the feelings of emptiness.**

Put another way: Do you want to spend a lifetime of being disconnected from your true self and purpose, or are you willing to undergo the psychic surgery that will restore your true identity? If you choose to remain disconnected, know that you are choosing a life sentence—you will never escape the pain. You will only cover it up for brief, fleeting moments, while you brew up more internal turmoil. The journey to healing will feel worse at first, as it will require you to delve deep down into the vortex of the original pain you suffered as a child, but as your wound heals, you will be lifted out of the maze.

The first step is to decide that you want to get out of the maze; the decision must be made by you, for you, and not for anyone else but you.

I invite you to imagine your life as you dreamt it before you stopped dreaming. Visualize a life of joy, free of addiction and its impact. Picture yourself waking up feeling excited about what the day has to offer. It's never too late to recapture the part of you that was born to have a life of meaning and purpose—with loving relationships, a career or other work about which you are passionate, and the ability to ride life's ups and downs. This life waits for you to embrace it, but first you need to see where you are.

The following questions will help you determine if you are in a maze of addiction.

Self-Evaluation Questionnaire

Identify Your Pattern

1. Do you feel that you are in a maze? If so, draw what your maze looks like, identifying each corridor you have traveled. Write in the center of the maze the wounds that have fueled the vortex and formed the invisible hole.
2. Are you willing to get out of the maze? If the answer is yes, start your journey now by answering the rest of the questions.
3. Describe the pattern that has kept you trapped or going back to the same addiction, or kept you from trying a new path.
4. List all your habits that you feel have gotten out of control.
5. How did you know you were out of control?

Identify Your Imprint

1. Describe your first crush: What features (color hair and eyes, height, shape, and so forth), have stuck in your mind? Describe the feelings of the first crush. Where did you feel it in your body? Did your face turn red? Were you nervous? Was your heart racing? Did you feel sexually aroused?

2. Have you carried that imprint forward in your romantic life? List the partner(s) you recall who match that original imprint.

3. Were you psychologically compatible with people who matched your imprint? Why or why not?

4. What areas of compatibility are the most important to you?

5. With whom was your most successful relationship? What made it that way?

6. Describe what you would consider to be a healthy relationship.

7. Which is more important to you: physical attraction or compatibility?

PART 3

ONE SOLUTION

Many experts believe that an addiction can't be cured; it can only be stopped. *Merriam-Webster Dictionary* defines *cure* as "recovery or relief from a disease."[1] If an addiction is an illness, or "disorder" as the *Diagnostic and Statistical Manual of Mental Disorders (DSM)* claims, it seems to me that "recovery or relief" from that condition would be a cure. Following that train of thought, it would also seem that when someone stops engaging in an addiction, the cure would be automatic—but we know this is not the case. Once people become addicted, they can never safely resume that behavior no matter the length of abstinence. So even though a cure is the absence of symptoms and many addicts have achieved this level of recovery, we will use the word *solution* to avoid the dispute over whether or not addiction can be cured.

We do not fully understand why someone who has become addicted can never safely resume that particular activity, but we do know that addicted people have lost the ability to predict what will happen when they re-engage. The unfortunate proof of this fact can be seen in the millions of people who have repeatedly tried to manage an addiction with occasional indulgence and have failed. Even those people who, after decades of abstinence, re-engaged in the addictive behavior ultimately came to find that they were as badly addicted, or worse, than before they quit. Even those who've had years of therapy and thought they were safe to dabble found out otherwise. Perhaps the cause is permanent brain change that science has failed to fully understand. Whether we use medical or psychological reasoning, we need to accept the fact that, once "recovered," addicts can never safely partake of the thing to which they were addicted.

Full recovery from addiction requires more than abstinence. My goal here is not to analyze why we cannot reverse an addiction. Instead, my goal is to show you a path beyond mere abstinence that leads straight to permanent remission—a solution.

Every addiction is a substitute for love, so once we replace the addictive act with an act of love, the desire to use anyone or anything will be gone.

9

LOVE IS THE ONLY SOLUTION

The greatest disease in the West today is not TB or leprosy;
it is being unwanted, unloved, and uncared for. . . .
There are many in the world who are dying for a piece of
bread but there are many more dying for a little love.

—Mother Teresa

People who love themselves don't want to self-destruct. When we understand this basic concept, addiction can be eradicated before it ever starts. If the billions of dollars thrown at fighting addiction could be turned into teaching the value of self-love—starting with parenting—the invisible hole would never form in the first place. But for those people already suffering from addiction, the solution is the same—love.

For our purposes, let's follow the definition that an illness (addiction) is cured as long as the person is asymptomatic. Along these lines, an addiction is no different than any other illness. Take cancer, for example; if a person is diagnosed and treated and is free of symptoms, that illness is in remission. You can remove a cancerous tumor from the lung of a smoker, but if the person continues to smoke, the cancer is likely to return. But if that person never smokes again and never encounters another bout with cancer, the person remains asymptomatic, and a full remission has occurred. By definition (relieved of symptoms), that person is cured.

Concerning addiction, you might be in remission (abstinent) from a particular addiction, but that doesn't mean your symptoms are gone. Just because a person isn't using doesn't mean the person is in recovery from addiction—the invisible hole will just look for another fix. You're recovered when you stop looking for anything to fill the emptiness.

Engaging in any addictive behavior is only one component of the illness. To get well, you must treat all the symptoms. The most important (and most often ignored) of all the symptoms is the emotional component—the mental obsession that creates each and every relapse is driven by the invisible hole.

> **People who love themselves don't want to self-destruct.**

Until the emotional wound is tended to and healed, no one is cured. Even if the behavior stops, the danger of relapse looms, and whenever someone or something bumps up against that wound, the trigger will set off the urge to self-medicate to ease the pain.

A case in point: Marshall went to Alcoholics Anonymous because his wife was concerned about his drinking. It wasn't enough that during the previous five years, he had been arrested for DUI, had lost two clients, and had an employee who quit, all because of his drinking. His denial about being addicted allowed him to compartmentalize those disasters as if they were unrelated occurrences. Like any person who is addicted, he was convinced he could manage his alcohol intake. He was physically fit, handsome, and well liked in the community. In spite of the problems his alcohol use had created, Marshall managed to recover from these setbacks and bounced back. He also had managed to earn his license as an insurance agent and achieve financial success. All these things kept his denial intact. Finally, after another DUI, his wife threatened to leave if he didn't get help. Given the choice of alcohol or his marriage, but only halfway convinced he had a problem, he reluctantly went to AA.

He stopped drinking, but his underlying wound remained. No longer able to lose himself in alcohol, he grew moody as he missed his nightly one or two bottles of wine. Marshall's wife was displeased with her (unhappy) sober husband and began to keep her distance. Thinking that giving up alcohol had been bad for him and his marriage, he resumed drinking, and, within months, found himself divorced and alone—but not for long.

Marshall rapidly got involved in a new relationship, and he continued to go on and off the wagon, reenacting the same pattern as with his wife. When his girlfriend threatened to break up with him, he would stop, then after a few months, he'd start again. At one point, Marshall's drinking became so bad, he landed in the hospital. This was his turning point. If he was to stay alive, he needed to stay sober, and to do that, he had to identify his wound and heal the pain template that propelled his self-destructive drinking.

Marshall had grown up an only child whose parents spent little time with him. He acknowledged that there was stability in his household, but he had few memories of warmth and family interaction. He recalled spending many hours alone in his bedroom, consumed with loneliness and a sense that he wasn't worth much to his parents. His low self-esteem made it difficult for him to make friends. His feeling that he was somehow defective followed him to college, where he drank alcohol for the first time and all his insecurities seemed magically to evaporate. While drinking, he felt confident and connected. Although he was primarily a social drinker, his new best friend, alcohol, never let him down; he joined a fraternity, got a girlfriend, and created a life he could call his own.

During the next thirty years, his "friend" turned into his enemy, as it slowly hijacked his mind. By age fifty, Marshall had a choice to make: either face that demon or allow it to claim his life. Marshall's wound was clear. Ever since college, whenever the unconscious feelings of loneliness or inferiority crept up on him, he drank. Abstinence offered sobriety but not relief. Each time the pain hit a certain threshold, he sought comfort in his addiction.

Anytime he felt a loved one pull away, he experienced overwhelming feelings of abandonment. When his wife had been distant, he'd become flooded with the old feelings of loneliness that he had endured throughout his childhood. Once Marshall stopped using alcohol, he found himself still stuck in the same teenage state of mental isolation he'd experienced before he started drinking. Once again, Marshall felt unable to make new friends, engage in new hobbies, or otherwise take care of himself by meeting his needs in healthy ways.

After his divorce, the same pattern continued with his girlfriend, as any perceived distance on her part triggered him again. The first glass of wine obliterated the void he felt within. He felt a brief sense of relief, but once the wine got into his system, it once again hijacked his mind, and he lost the ability to stop. Until he addressed the core cause of his pain, he would be governed by that relentless force that would precede his first drink.

During his last binge, Marshall had become so addicted to alcohol that he could not stop drinking long enough to leave his apartment. He drank until he passed out at night, woke up with the shakes, and had to pour himself another drink to function. His drinking had gone the full progression, from anxiety relief to negative consequences, to complete physical addiction and withdrawal. Fortunately, at this point Marshall called someone he'd met in AA and asked for help. Marshall became open to the possibility that something deep within him needed to be addressed, and he agreed to return to AA meetings. He also agreed to therapy so he could excavate and heal the wounds of his past that continued to drive his addiction.

During the next year, Marshall was able to stay sober while he ventured into the invisible hole and properly grieved. With each healed memory, he filled his hole with self-love—releasing pain through tears, allowing himself to be comforted, abstaining from harmful behaviors, substituting addiction with a healthy lifestyle—nutrition, exercise, spirituality, and friends. As the void diminished and he became more authentic, he grew closer to himself and those around him.

It's been five years since Marshall had his last drink. He's gone on to live a full life, enjoying a rewarding career, friendships, hobbies, and travel. The last time I saw Marshall, he told me he wouldn't drink again even if he could.

"The thought of putting alcohol in my body doesn't appeal to me anymore; it poisoned me to the point it almost killed me. Strange. Until I had realized that I drank for sorrow rather than pleasure, I was never going to get better. Once I dealt with all the sadness, there was never a good enough reason to pick up the first drink." From that point forward, Marshall's reactions were no longer rooted in his past, and as long as he continues to take care of himself, Marshall can consider himself cured from alcoholism.

Another patient, Elaine, came to therapy for severe depression. She'd been diagnosed with breast cancer and had undergone a mastectomy and chemotherapy. She was in remission, but the life-threatening experience had opened the floodgates of pain that she'd carried with her since early childhood. When she came to therapy, she told me that she wanted to die, but she could not kill herself because she feared her children would be devastated.

When Elaine was five, she'd been told by her father that she was the result of an unplanned pregnancy; shortly thereafter, he died. Elaine adopted the belief that somehow her being born had caused his death. Unable to assuage her own guilt, she could not mourn her father's death. Her guilty feelings and sense of being unwanted were compounded when her mother had to work long hours to pay the bills, and she and her two siblings were left to care for themselves. Several times during her childhood, Elaine had been sent to stay with an aunt who was cold toward her and with whom she did not feel welcomed.

Her aunt, deeply involved in her church, brought Elaine to religious services several times each week where she was instructed to adhere to Old Testament principles or face the wrath of God. Elaine's aunt home-schooled her through junior high and high school.

At age eighteen, Elaine married a man she'd met at church, and they had three children. Overwhelmed with childcare, unhappy in her marriage, and feeling under the control of an oppressive deity, Elaine hoarded candy bars and chocolate that she would binge on when her family was asleep. Eating sweets became her way to cope.

Elaine's life was spent in silent suffering as her world revolved around family and church, neither of which she felt she ever freely chose; they had been imposed on her by an aunt who wanted to be freed from the responsibility of caring for Elaine. It wasn't until she faced a medical crisis with breast cancer at age fifty that a lifetime of pent-up pain and frustration descended upon her.

Even though Elaine had survived successful surgery and treatment, she fell into a deep depression. Food and her grown children were the only remaining pleasures she had that could help soothe her pain template. Since all her children lived out of town, Elaine mostly turned to food. She lived to eat, and her husband made sure she was well fed, ordering pizza, soda, ice cream, and all their other favorite comfort foods—their only remaining connection.

Once again, Elaine felt trapped. She did not want to remain married to a man she did not love, but she would not allow herself to think of an alternative without reliving the same guilt she felt for believing she'd killed her father. She now believed getting cancer was a punishment from God for the (imagined) sin of killing her father.

As part of her therapy, she begrudgingly agreed to go to 12-Step meetings to address her food addiction. She began to make new friends and found a connection to a higher power that made sense to her—with a loving God, not a wrathful one. As her depression slowly lifted and her fear of being punished subsided, Elaine became ready to do the deeper work that would free her from the pain still driving her eating disorder and guilt.

As she moved through the layers of childhood grief at the center of her pain vortex, she began to see how her feelings of guilt over her father's death had caused her to feel unworthy. Free of guilt, she was able to grieve the loss of her father and the absence of a childhood with a unified family. Once the pain of her past left her, the need to medicate her grief with sugar subsided. Six months into therapy, Elaine had lost weight, was re-engaged with life, and had removed the cloak of shame that had kept her with a man with whom she no longer wished to live. Sharing her true feelings for the first time, Elaine was able to feel love for herself and her husband without it having to be romantic. Elaine's honesty with herself and her husband enabled them to form an authentic connection. Her husband began to understand Elaine's suffering and was able to let her go. They remained close friends even after their separation.

Healing Takes Courage

You might be thinking that one or both of these cases sounds too good to be true, and you might doubt that either person could break lifelong habits so easily. You should. I want you to know that it wasn't easy for either one of them. In fact, both people, and all the others who've gotten out of the maze, had to muster all their strength and brave their way into the vortex of unresolved pain that kept the invisible hole an open wound. As inner work or therapy brings you closer to the wound that formed the invisible hole in the first place, the tendency of most people is to hesitate—many turn back.

> Choosing love over fear means giving up the illusion
> that you won't enjoy yourself without your addiction.

If you want to be released from the prison of addiction and get out of the maze forever, you can, but you've got to be willing to confront the unresolved trauma and pain that caused the invisible hole to form and learn how to fill that hole with self-love. I am going to guide you through the process step-by-step. But before we do that, there are some ground rules.

The first step to choosing love over fear is to decide to stop doing hateful things to yourself (addictive behavior) and to commit to choosing love over fear when the opportunity presents itself. I want you to think of addiction like any other bad relationship. You might get some fleeting benefit or pleasure, but the price you pay is awful. Before getting over any type of relationship, you have to tell it goodbye, feel the grief, and move on. Moving on means doing something good for you in place of doing something harmful.

Choosing love over fear means giving up the illusion that you won't enjoy your life without your addiction. Loving yourself means you stop whatever is making you sick no matter how much you've been brainwashed into thinking that you enjoy that particular thing. You will make yourself remember how awful your first taste of alcohol or tobacco was, how you felt when you lost at gambling, the guilt associated with violating your own moral and sexual standards, the exhaustion you felt from working too hard, or how sick you felt from eating too much sugar. Consider the possibility that you do not enjoy something that is destroying you and your self-esteem, and that is harming those around you. Ask yourself honestly whether a few moments of pleasure are worth the price you pay for that brief escape.

The Difference Between Feeling Love and Feeling High

Love is one of the most discussed and most misunderstood words in the world. If you are to ever recover, you must distinguish between love and all its substitutes.

What does it mean to love yourself? Unfortunately, many people have equated love with a feeling they get when they do something they like: "I love chocolate chip cookies." "I love to go to the casino." "I love to drink expensive champagne." "I love sex." "I love to smoke pot." "I love pizza." "I love cigarettes." "I love to go shopping." These experiences create a sense of euphoria, but they are not love. They are rituals that have been implanted in our brains and get us high, but they are not love.

Love is not a feeling. Love is an action. Love is a state of being. It is being in a place of fullness and abundance and acting from a consciousness of love.

Think about it like this: You are a new parent, and your newborn starts crying in the middle of the night. You've just laid down after a hard day's work, and you're exhausted. You wish the baby would go back to sleep, and you'd like just to yell, "Go back to sleep!" But instead, you drag yourself out of bed and tend to the baby's needs. This is love. You don't give the child a drug or a cookie; you address the need appropriately. You don't feel like getting up, but you pull from something deep inside yourself, where love is, and tend to that helpless infant.

> **Loving yourself means caring for yourself in a way that honors your mind, body, and spirit.**

The same formula applies to you. When you are hungry, you eat healthy food. When you are tired, you rest. When you are sad, you cry. When you are angry, you talk about it. When you are sick, you take care of yourself. When you are lonely, you seek companionship. You can eat, drink, smoke, and otherwise anesthetize yourself, but that won't provide the right supplement for the problem. When you love yourself (or someone else), you do things that you don't feel like doing, and then the good feelings come. Instead of the quick-fix high of feeling temporarily good, you are learning how to feel good about yourself—permanently.

First, loving yourself means caring for yourself in a way that honors your mind, body, and spirit, which means caring for your mental, physical, and spiritual health. It might take a little while to notice the shift, but once you stop engaging in self-destructive behaviors and replace them with healthy ones, you will begin to see what you've been missing. You will begin to understand what healthy love looks and feels like. Plus, you'll be so busy enjoying life, you won't be thinking about the addiction other than feeling grateful that it's only something you used to do.

Second, to choose love over fear means you will keep taking care of yourself no matter what—no matter how bad you feel, no matter what discomfort you need to endure, no matter how many times you fail—you will keep on practicing loving yourself and never give up. Never.

You see, nothing will ever help you if you are not willing to learn how to love yourself. The only true replacement for addiction is to learn self-love. Rather than "treating" yourself with ice cream or wine, you can learn to relish truly loving behaviors, such as being gentle with yourself, forgiving yourself and others for mistakes, and treating your body like a sacred temple.

Love is the only thing that will give you the courage to revisit the pain that perpetuates the invisible hole and helps you stay there until you heal the emotional wound(s) and the pain is gone. Once that wound is healed and you replace it with self-love, the thought of destroying yourself with addictive behavior or any unloving act will no longer hold an allure.

Once again, you will treat your pain as if you're a small child and the loving adult at the same time. You will nurse those wounds, hug yourself, and cry until all the sadness is gone.

There is only one cure for addiction, one way out of the maze, and that is loving yourself. Maybe, like so many of us, you don't yet know what true love feels like because your pain template taught you otherwise. You may be afraid to investigate your past and the point where addiction took hold. But you don't have to worry about being hurt again by your past; it's over. The only important thing for you to do now is to learn to love yourself, and the first step is to honor yourself by choosing love over fear.

There is only one cure for addiction, one way out of the maze, and that is loving yourself.

Self-Evaluation Questionnaire

Identify Ways to Love Yourself

1. List a time or two in your life when you felt courageous.
2. What are some things that you say you love that haven't been good for you?

3. Make a list of all the substitutes you've used for love—food, alcohol, sex, thrills, and so forth.
4. Do you feel you've ever compromised yourself in the name of love? Did that make you feel better or worse about yourself?
5. What are three ways you can show yourself love now?

CHOOSE LOVE OVER FEAR

Perfect love casts out fear. If fear exists,
then there is not perfect love.
—*A Course in Miracles*

When I was newly sober, I embarked on a hard-core search for a spiritual connection that I'd always longed for but had never cultivated. I'd always enjoyed going to church, but I couldn't fully surrender there no matter how many attempts I made. I felt that traditional religion promoted fear over love, and I just couldn't buy into something my intuition told me was incorrect. I'd read the Bible and thought if God, our creator, was love, how could we all be evil sinners who need to be punished? And if the primary instruction, going as far back as Moses, was to love God and to treat one another well, and it was later reinforced by Jesus to love God, love one another, and love ourselves, how did religion take us so far off track? Since when did guidance on how to live a life of respect for our creator, parents, spouse, and neighbors degrade to institutionalized shame and guilt over human frailty?

One day, while sharing these thoughts over a cup of coffee with a friend, she told me I'd probably like *A Course in Miracles*. She hadn't studied it herself, but from what she knew, she thought it might be a solution for me, and she let me know that I could get a copy at the local Unity Church. The next day, as I thumbed through the pages of the course—the most compelling book I'd ever held—all I could think was, Yes, yes, yes. For me, it was like jumping into a swimming pool on a hot summer's day, and though my spiritual quest has taken me the world over, in my mind, nothing has come close to what I learned in this book.

A Course in Miracles was written by Helen Schucman, PhD, a professor of medical psychology at the Columbia-Presbyterian Medical Center

in New York City. Troubled by the overwhelming conflicts in her depart-
ment, she and her colleague, William Thetford, PhD, agreed that "there
must be a better way" of addressing conflicts and differences among the
staff.[1] Shortly thereafter, Schucman, an atheist, was guided by an inner
voice to start writing.[2] The resulting work was *A Course in Miracles*.

The course includes a text, 365 daily exercises, and a teacher's manual.
Thetford assisted Schucman's transcription, and later, a fellow psychoanalyst, Kenneth Wapnick, PhD, facilitated its editing and publication by
the Foundation for Inner Peace.

According to the course, the concept of a miracle is different than
what we're accustomed to. Instead of miraculous physical healing, the
healing is in the mind. A miracle occurs when we perceive through love
instead of fear. The result is a happier mental state and consequently, better all around health. For example, if I'm frustrated with my friend because
she hasn't called me in weeks, I could change my perception. I could reach
out to her. I could cultivate time with someone else. I could decide that
there's something positive from this disconnect and I can either attempt
to heal it or walk away. The course warns us that when we become disappointed and separate, we are acting from fear instead of love.

Given the current global political polarization as I write this, we could
all use some miracle-minded thinking.

Before I go on, I'd like to take a moment to clarify something important. Many people confuse *A Course in Miracles* with Marianne Williamson,
mistaking her as the author. Williamson is not the author; she is a student
of the course, who has received national recognition through her lectures
and course-related books.

The teachings of the course have brought immeasurable healing to me
and my relationships. Through its teachings, I've stopped blaming anyone
or anything for my problems, experienced more forgiveness and vulnerability, and learned how to replace my fears with love. I credit my (mostly)
constant state of happiness and joy to the many hours of therapeutic healing and spiritual connection *A Course in Miracles* has provided me.

In my opinion, people like Martin Luther King Jr. provide excellent
examples of people who have impacted the world through love. Though
they were not course students, or perfect, they exemplify what it teaches.
They spoke for unity without attacking their oppressors. Their messages

inspired, rather than condemned. Such individuals created massive change through *being what they taught*, through inspiration rather than fear. This is the vital message of *A Course in Miracles*. It encourages us to look beyond the flaws of every human and to recognize that within every person is perfect love. While human flaws are apparent, we can appeal to the divine aspect in each person. When we live this way, there is no need to attack.

A Course in Miracles is a psychological/spiritual course that, in my opinion, refines psychoanalytic concepts while also renewing the teachings of Jesus that urged people to connect inwardly with God instead of relying on a religious institution for that connection. Keep in mind, Helen Schucman was a psychologist, educated in psychoanalysis, and an atheist without a religious agenda. This combination made her an exceptional candidate for channeling the course's psychological contents without having a religious-based mental block on the spiritual concepts.

The course teaches that within every human is a deeper consciousness, the "Holy Spirit," and the course defines human consciousness as the "ego." The Holy Spirit is based in love; the ego is fear-based and keeps us stuck in an unloving mindset toward ourselves and others.

The course's definition of ego is different from the ego that Freud introduced. Freud postulated that the ego was a part of the personality that served as a fulcrum balancing impulses and drives (the id) with an overly moral conscience (superego). The course's reference to ego is a combination of the id that wants immediate gratification and a superego that then shames you for indulging. The purpose of this ego is to create constant chaos and separate us from love. It finds fault instead of what's good about someone. It tells us to throw all caution aside and do what it takes to get what we want. Then as soon as we achieve the goal, the ego is not satisfied and starts looking for the next conquest. It convinces us to get even with whoever hurts us. It tries to separate us from people who love us. The ego does all this is the name of protecting us or to feel better about ourselves (fear of being unloved).

> Since addiction at its core is a substitute for love, it's clear why love is the only solution.

The course's definition of ego is one that forms out of a painful environment. As we've previously covered, when children's needs are met, they view the world as a satisfying place of fulfillment. If the childhood is full of unresolved hurt, then the pain template is transferred beyond the family and projected onto the grown child's expectations in the world. When this happens, the child's damaged ego seeks only to escape pain and find substitutes for love. This is the precursor for addiction. Since addiction at its core is a substitute for love, it's clear why love is the only solution.

The Holy Spirit is the aspect of us that is not physical but eternal and is one with the creator. Rather than God being some force that cannot be touched and felt, the course teaches us that the Holy Spirit is the pipeline to God. As we practice listening to and following the inner guidance of that loving voice, we begin to see our lives change for the better. With time, a sense of trust and self-love grows from having that conscious contact with this innate spiritual part of ourselves.

The purpose of *A Course in Miracles* is to teach us how to choose love (listen to the Holy Spirit) over fear (heeding the whims of the ego). I realize that some people take issue with words such as *God* and *Spirit*, so if you don't like those terms, use the word *love*. Or some people just use the word *conscience* and then later realize it's the voice of love. You can practice listening to the loving voice inside of you no matter what you choose to call it.

While this might be a new concept to you, the course would say you already know everything that it offers; you have simply forgotten it because you've been taught otherwise. The course explains that throughout life, your fearful ego was conditioned by an unsafe environment. You were rewarded for "good" behavior and punished for "bad" behavior. Children raised this way learn that a person can be lovable only if they follow all the rules—a concept quite different than teaching a child they are lovable no matter what, and that loving acts bring forth good feelings, and unloving behaviors lower self-esteem. Teaching children to make decisions based on loving themselves and others requires a conscious effort on the part of role models; it's not as expedient as negative reinforcement or punishment, but it is one that yields many long-term rewards.

Some religions teach people to stop "sinning" so they can stay out of hell. The course teaches us that we are already in hell when we are governed by the ego. Remember, according to the course's definition, the primary purpose of the ego is to separate us from love. When we are governed by the fear-based ego, we become so miserable that we make choices that take us toward death over life. The Holy Spirit teaches us how to love ourselves and share love with and receive love from others. When we do this, like the rats in the Rat Park (see chapter 6) experiment, we are too busy enjoying our lives to be consumed with addiction.

The course teaches that even though the ego governs by fear, the fear is hidden behind guilt and anger. Anger pushes people away. Guilt and shame make people feel bad for what they do, but they rarely change a person's behavior. Addicts keep using whether or not they feel guilty or ashamed.

I'd also like to add that *A Course in Miracles* does not specifically address anxiety. I believe that *anxiety* is just another word for *fear*. When patients start labeling their anxiety as fear, they begin to get a new sense of personal power by walking through the fear, as opposed to learning how to "manage" anxiety.

> Even though the ego governs by fear,
> the fear is hidden behind guilt and anger.

The course does not refer to a healthy conscience but to guilt, which keeps us stuck in an unloving mindset toward ourselves, and we don't change a thing. Nor does the course teach that anger is bad; it simply reminds us it's a cover-up for fear. Once the fear is exposed, the anger goes away. However, when someone is violating you or your rights, feeling angry is natural, and when we love ourselves, we don't allow people to walk all over us. Expressing yourself honestly yet kindly is choosing love. For example, if your loved one has repeatedly lied to you, once you've addressed your fear, you could say, "I'm feeling confused about the inconsistencies in your story. I could be wrong, but it seems you're not always honest with me. Trust is very important to me. When I'm lied to, I don't feel safe."

Misplaced or poorly managed anger due to ego-based fear of rejection or confrontation means that conflicts are approached through either direct or indirect attacks. Getting even (passive-aggression), secretly doing the same behavior, bad-mouthing people behind their back but never bringing your concerns to them directly are examples of indirect attacks.

Outright blame and verbal abuse are two examples of direct attacks. Both are equally unloving toward yourself and others. The course emphasizes that when acting out in anger rather than dealing with the fear underneath anger and guilt, we project it onto another person. When we learn to ask ourselves what we fear, instead of what we feel angry or guilty about, we change the course of our lives. Such an inquiry restores our inner power and allows us to face the unconscious fear that has been driving us. Then we are able to provide ourselves with the loving parenting we needed as children but didn't receive enough of or in the right way, and can walk ourselves through our emotional blocks.

> **When we love ourselves, we can learn how to make our way out of any hellhole and into a life of joy.**

When making life decisions, to which voice will you listen? Love (Holy Spirit) or fear (ego)? As I'm writing this book, I hear both voices. My ego constantly tells me that I'm opening myself up to public humiliation. I imagine every embarrassing moment of my life being aired in living color for the world to see. The other voice tells me not to worry about all that; the only thing I need to focus on is helping others, not concerning myself with made-up fears. If stories of my past can be used to help others out of the maze, then so be it.

When we love ourselves, we can learn how to make our way out of any hellhole and into a life of joy.

We are not expected to digest the course teachings overnight, as they are a whole new way of thinking. When I teach the course, I tell students to think of it as learning a new language; it takes time and practice. You cannot pick up a French book and speak fluent French on your first try. You need guidance and practice, and the more you work with it, the faster you learn.

On the following pages, I'm going to lead you through the steps that have healed many people of their addiction. Please keep in mind that you are not being graded, and it's okay to make mistakes. I've never seen anyone go from living a life of addiction to a life of self-love overnight. Expect it to take time, practice, and patience. Each time you choose love over fear, you are tending to a long-ignored wound, and given enough time, you can heal it.

As you practice choosing love over fear, you can begin to see the difference between treating yourself with love and abusing yourself with addiction. Just because your childhood formed a pain template doesn't mean you have to keep associating pain with pleasure. Even though the ego says that by indulging in your addiction, you are treating yourself to some type of reward, try to remember that your so-called "reward" is a substitute for authentic love—and a poor one at that. Addiction is taking much more from you than the temporary fix it offers. Each time you get that one hit, you pay a painful price. Your self-esteem diminishes as your money, your loved ones, your health, and ultimately your life, slips away to addiction.

Here's how the ego orchestrates addiction. Let's take cigarettes. Your doctor tells you that you have to quit smoking. It's ruining your health. Outside pressure rarely works when stopping addiction—stopping must come from the desire to love yourself. When the pressure is external, the ego remains in control.

Automatically, the ego starts putting up a force of resistance: *It's too hard to quit smoking. You've tried it so many times before. You know you're going to be miserable. You'll hate it. You'll miss your cigarettes. You know how much you love to smoke. So what are you going to do? You'll gain weight again. Cigarettes are your best friend.* And so on.

At any point, you could ask yourself, "Who's voice is that?" But instead, you listen to it, and it wears you down. But now, for health reasons, you must stop. So your ego brings up its second line of defense.

Okay, you have to quit, but let's wait until after your birthday. You know you'll be miserable at your party if you can't smoke. Then after your birthday's over, *'Let's wait until the weekend. Oh no! The dog is sick. If the dog dies, you'll start again, so let's wait to make sure the dog is all right first. Well, you can't exactly stop smoking during the holidays. You know you'll eat too many sweets when you stop smoking. You'll get fat. The holidays are the worst time to quit smoking. Definitely on the first. Yes, January 1.*

It's now been ten months since you decided to quit smoking. Finally, after a few more delays, you are ready to stop. It's January 10. You've disposed of all your cigarettes and told everyone you're quitting. You're done. The next day you have your coffee, and your ego reminds you, *I love coffee with my cigarettes.* You shrug it off. A few hours later, you get the tap on the shoulder, *I want a cigarette.* You ignore it. You feel pretty good about yourself. You've made it eight hours without smoking. After dinner, more tapping, *This is your favorite time to relax and have a smoke. Look, Jerry over there is smoking. Why not just take a puff of his?* You resist. You make it through the whole day.

You make it through two more days listening to the relentless ego say, *I want a cigarette.* It's hard. Then you have one of those days from hell.

Everything goes wrong. You're angry and disappointed in someone or something. You feel like you're coming unglued. The ego is right there with you. *I want a cigarette. It would make me feel so much better.* The demand is so incessant that the ego is like a two-year-old stomping their foot. *I want a cigarette! I want a cigarette! I want a cigarette! Please, just one, I only want one. Just give me one, and I promise to be good.*

Soon after that, the pack of cigarettes is in hand. You rip off the package, light one up. You deeply inhale, the nicotine hits your brain, and it feels like you're in heaven again—your best friend's back. You throw the rest of the pack away. You're okay. You're in control. *See, I told you, you could have just one.*

The next day you buy another pack, but when you're about to throw the rest away, *You really shouldn't throw the pack away. It's too expensive. Let's give it away.* While deciding who gets the pack, three more cigarettes are gone. *Look, let's just do three a day, that won't hurt anyone—one with coffee, one after lunch, and one after dinner.*

After a few days of controlled smoking, *Now you're out of cigarettes again. What's the point anyhow? You haven't stopped. Let's get one more pack, just smoke three a day, and when this pack is gone, we'll definitely stop.* Before long, you're back up to a pack a day. And then the resignation that you can't quit is followed by condemnation. *I told you that you couldn't stop. You're too weak. You can't live without smoking. You'd have a week now if you hadn't started again after three days. How stupid. What are you going to tell everyone? They'll be so disappointed. You can just sneak them, only smoke outside of the house . . .*

This ego-thought process applies to any addiction. It's all the same: codependency, food, gambling, addictive relationships, sex, spending, sugar—it doesn't matter.

You could challenge the ego at any point, but that's not what's happening. That's why we must replace the ego with the voice of love. First, you quit because you want your mind and your life back. You realize you've been kidnapped and don't want to live like a slave anymore. You stop for *you*. You pick a date, and you meet the resistance with love. *My birthday is the best time to quit. It will be the best present I can give myself. Rather than thinking how hard it is, I will enjoy being free from this net that's cast over me. You're not my friend, and you're not invited to my birthday party or any other day of my life. Friends don't secretly destroy you.*

Whenever I want a cigarette, I'm going to do something else instead— like a new hobby, work a puzzle, make some delicious healthy appetizers for dinner, plant some flowers, go for a walk, call a friend, or go to a Smokers Anonymous meeting. I'm going to download an app that keeps track of how many days I live without you and how much money I'm saving. Smoking isn't heaven. It's hell. It's poisoning me. My body is sacred. My lungs are going to turn pink again. I can breathe again. I don't have to keep worrying about dying of lung disease.

If I smell cigarettes or see someone smoking, I won't judge, I'll just be happy smoking is something I don't do any more.

I'm addiction-free, and look at how much money I'm saving instead of buying cigarettes. There's a reason you can't just buy a few cigarettes at a time. They want you to stay addicted. I will put the cigarette money in a jar and save up for something on my dream list. I'm going to enjoy the fresh smell of my home and clothes. I'm not worried about replacing cigarettes with another addiction. I'm actually losing weight from all the healthy meals I prepare and vigorous strolls in the park.

People who love me are celebrating with me. Every time I feel upset, I'm going to tell cigarettes goodbye. I'm going to feel my feelings. I can do this without putting deadly toxins in my body. I wasn't born smoking. I'm not a smoker. I'm going to thank my higher power daily for helping me with this. I'm not going to worry about tomorrow, I'm going to enjoy today. That's all I have.

Most important, I will tell myself all the good things I need to hear. I'm going to build myself up, not tear myself down.

When working with someone, I tell them to think of the voice of love and the voice of the ego as two radio stations. One is the addiction/ego station. The other is the freedom/love station. Of course, the person has the choice to change the station at any time.

As you become more connected to your true self and the spiritual aspect of your mind, any form of abuse, from yourself or others, will lose its allure. The more you relate to yourself with love (from the Holy Spirit), the less fear will have a hold on you. You will begin to see the insanity of listening to your ego when it tells you to do something self-destructive— and it will lose its grip on you.

As you proceed further into your healing, notice how your addiction and the ego work in tandem: the ego will try to convince you it's okay to do something, saying, "Lighten up. Go ahead and have another drink, eat more ice cream, have another affair, place another bet; you deserve this." But the minute the high is over and the consequences hit you, the ego rapidly condemns you for doing the very thing it convinced you to do, asking, "Why did you do that, you stupid idiot? When will you learn?!" Did you catch that? Your ego talks you into doing something that's not good for you and then that same voice condemns you for so doing. This is how the ego keeps you in the maze and blocks you from seeing that you are addicted. It keeps convincing you that you can fill the invisible hole with things that really only dig it deeper. The first time you are able to tell that voice no and give yourself love instead, you will have begun the miraculous journey of being cured of addiction.

A Course in Miracles teaches us that the ego's goal is death, and the Holy Spirit's goal is a joyful life. This is almost identical to Freud's description of Thanatos (the God of death), every person's death wish, and Eros (the God of love), every person's wish for love. Through his work treating trauma, Freud wanted us to understand that there is a part of the mind that has a death instinct and a part of the mind that has a life instinct; they work in opposition to one another, and each instinct is driven by sex and aggression. It is beyond the scope of this book to elaborate on Freud's theories other than to explain that these competing drives often collide, and aggression can be turned inward, resulting in depression and suicidal behavior.

As you go through the following recommendations, be aware of the natural human (ego) tendency to ignore or resist the tools that are offered to help you heal your wounds. Remember that the ego wants you to separate from life, and it uses addiction as a weapon against you. Think about it—the more you engage in an addiction, the more isolated you become. The more you withdraw, the more you feel the invisible hole, and the more you crave the addiction. The vicious cycle pulls you further into the vortex, making it harder and harder to get out.

Love Requires Action

Love is not just a feeling. It is an action, and it take courage to change— even when it will be good for you.

Let love in. Let love cast out your fear and anything else that has blocked you from loving yourself. Don't give up; even if you doubt that you're getting better, know that you are. Pretend you are in the gym of spirituality. You can look in the mirror after many workouts and not see the change, but after a month or two, you can notice that your clothes fit more loosely, that you're more toned, and that your skin has a healthy glow. Spend as much time in loving yourself as you did in your addiction, and you will get rapid results.

> Love is not just a feeling. It is an action.

You may think that indulging in an addiction is being nice to yourself. It's not. Most addicted patients tell me that right before they partook, they told themselves they "deserved" to do whatever it was they weren't supposed to do. Many addicts have used their addiction as a reward for withstanding stress or emotional pain or for achieving a goal. But what the addict does not realize is that in that moment of deciding to use, the so-called reward is actually punishment in disguise. Anyone can prove this to themselves by asking a few simple questions: Is this thing I'm about to do actually good for me? What happened the last five times I did this? Did I feel better or worse after the pleasure wore off?

Dousing any form of discontent with an addiction will never make it go away. And drowning a celebration in booze never made the achievement greater either. I want to reiterate a point made earlier: addiction gives us the illusion that we feel good, all the while widening the invisible hole with more regret and suffering, fueling the vortex and burying us alive.

Every addictive behavior is a choice of fear over love. Hard to believe? Consider—what's the first thing that crosses your mind when you want to engage in your addiction? Doesn't the thought (from the ego) occur to you that if you don't partake, you won't like the way you feel? Isn't that fear of not feeling okay without your vice the very thing that tells you to go ahead regardless of the consequences? If you think your addiction's temporary high is offering you anything other than short-term relief in exchange for long-term emotional and physical torture, you are definitely on the road to death, not life.

Every addiction is a substitute for love. If you substitute love for addiction you will forget about addiction.

> **Drowning a celebration in booze never made the achievement greater.**

When I tried to stop smoking for the umpteenth time, one of the healers from whom I sought help asked me why it was so hard for me to stop. "Because I love cigarettes; they have been my best friend ever since I was twelve years old." She compassionately looked into my eyes and replied, "When you can say you love yourself as much as you love cigarettes, you won't want to poison yourself anymore."

Once that thought took hold, I was free from smoking, but it didn't take long for the hole inside of me to look for another place to fill up. I started long-distance bicycling, then running, thinking they were good for me, but I later realized the endorphins I obtained from the intensive exercise were the real reason I was running marathons—just another way to fill the same invisible hole.

Don't get me wrong, exercise is a good and loving behavior, but there a big difference between moderate and extreme exercise. I was going for the high more than anything else and didn't even realize I was robbing myself of good self-esteem. The goal isn't to replace a bad addiction with a healthier one but instead to replace all addictions with balanced, healthy, loving behaviors.

My quest for love's substitutes continued for many years. Until I realized there was nothing outside of me that could ever offer the fulfillment I sought, I was only exchanging one addiction for another.

A Course in Miracles taught me that my ego would keep searching but never find what I was looking for. There is no substitute for love. The course taught me that I had not found the peace I so desperately sought because it wasn't out there; it was within me.

Underneath every addiction is a desire to replace an unwanted feeling with a better one. The only problem is, it doesn't work. We reach for something, and sure enough, we get that momentary relief, but it quickly fades away to the unquenchable thirst for more. When the addiction stops, the good feeling of being alive can return.

Remember, what we fail to realize is that we *fear* the feelings that will come up when we make the choice of not using. *If I don't do this, I will feel worse than I do now* is the unconscious thought that precedes using. The (fearful) thought of deprivation or loss propels the addict to keep doing the very thing that creates more discomfort and more loss. Then guilt for succumbing to the addiction keeps the person stuck, feeling powerless and worthless.

Like the rats in the experiment we discussed earlier, when we are addicted, we push the lever to get the quick hit without realizing that the more we push that lever, the more we actually lose. When we are addicted, we run deeper into the maze on autopilot, following the navigation of the ego telling us we ought to do something that isn't good for us. We never stop to question it.

You don't have to do this anymore. There is a way out.

| Self-Evaluation Questionnaire

Identify the Cover-up for Love

1. How would you define *love?*
2. How would you define *fear?*

3. Has guilt governed you? What are some of the things you feel guilty about? Has your guilt permanently stopped you from breaking free of an unwanted pattern?

4. When you feel angry, what do you do? Shut down? Yell? How do you feel after you have either swallowed or blasted out your anger?

5. Is there something you fear missing if you give it up?

6. Does the thought of love scare you? If so, why?

7. Have you ever felt loved, even briefly? If so, describe that/those experience(s).

8. If your life were full of love, what would that look like?

9. If you have a particular addictive behavior, what could you replace it with?

STEP ONE TOWARD LOVE— REMOVE THE BARRIERS

Pain is inevitable. Suffering is optional.

—**Anonymous**

Feelings are at the root of every addiction. In this chapter, we are going to confront, address, and forgive years of pent-up feelings and unaddressed pain, and you will read about ways to embrace your feelings and express them. It can be confusing to hear that you need to embrace your feelings but manage them at the same time. This can seem unnatural to learn as an adult, especially if you've spent a lifetime trying to ignore your feelings, stuff them down, or snuff them out.

Your feelings are a healthy part of you, and how you address them and express them can either be a benefit or a detriment to yourself and those around you. All feelings contain important signals and information. The most empowered choice you can make is to use your feelings as a guide for healing and *not let your feelings use you* to the point that you hurt yourself or others. As you read on, think of your feelings as your gateway to healing and know that how you express those feelings can become the loving evidence of your healing.

Yes, it's hard to face things that happened in your past, to take an honest look at what might have been missing in your family of origin, or to give up a rosy illusion of a perfect family. But again, this isn't about blame; it's about facing the truth to reach a clear understanding, so you can sort out the reasons your invisible hole was formed. Maybe your childhood wasn't so bad, but a crisis caused you trauma and pain. If you engaged in an addiction, you unknowingly created a self-inflicted trauma brought on by regret, hurting others, physical harm and violating your own moral standards. Armed with the facts, you don't have to blame yourself or anyone else; you simply put the pieces together to create a better understanding of how the addiction took root in the first place. With that knowledge comes the power to break the emotional patterns that precipitated your addiction.

> **Your feelings are a healthy part of you, and how you address them and express them can either be a benefit or a detriment.**

Before you begin, I want to caution you. The process is so simple, you might be inclined to ignore it. Many people get this far, and they think they don't actually need to follow the steps because they're so obvious, so easy. But just because it's easy doesn't mean it's comfortable. It's like getting a cavity repaired. You can put it off as long as you want, but the decay and subsequent pain only get worse. Once the dentist has treated your tooth, you wonder why you ignored the problem for so long. Don't be like I was at first and think you already know how to practice. You can read a book on how to fly a plane, but good luck with actual takeoff and landing. Equally important, these are lifetime exercises—that means you will need to practice them forever. The more you practice, the more skilled you become. You're worth the investment. Stay with it; don't stop.

First Barrier: Face the Pain

Underneath every addiction is old, unaddressed pain. That pain is a wall that keeps you isolated and lonely. Unless that wall of pain is removed, it will keep love out. You probably don't even realize there is a wall because your addiction has cleverly hidden that truth from you. It's told you that you only need *it*—not people or anything else to love. Fear might have told you people aren't worth the effort, so you just gave up on trying. Fear might have said to you that to love is too painful, so you closed your heart to the warmth of connection. But once you learn how to love yourself, fear will no longer dictate your decisions, and you will be free.

As we discussed earlier, even if you have a genetic predisposition, you weren't born addicted. Something happened that created that invisible hole. If you find yourself addicted, know that despite your efforts to avoid discomfort and find pleasure, you have found pain. You might think this sounds crazy, but I assure you it's true. Let's take alcohol as an example. Imagine you had a bad day at work and came home feeling stressed, so you pour yourself a glass of wine, kick off your shoes, sit in your favorite chair, and think with great satisfaction, *Ah! After such a terrible day, I deserve this!*

Fast-forward to when you wake up the next morning still in your favorite chair but with a raging headache, two empty bottles and cocaine wrappers on the floor beside you. Now you are experiencing pain and have set yourself up for another bad day at work—if you can make it there at all. This example illustrates the illusion that perpetuates the addiction loop, but I could have used any addiction pattern to make this point—bingeing on your favorite food, going on a shopping spree you can't afford, watching porn instead of having sex with your partner, gambling your entire paycheck. No matter what substance or activity you choose, the pattern is the same. You turn to the addictive behavior to deal with pain or the void in your life, and as a result, you succeed only in creating more pain and more emptiness, and you don't even realize why. I believe that every addiction reaction is a call for an equal and opposite loving action. If you're addicted, this signifies that you've gone to great lengths to avoid your emotions, and you probably never realized the extent to which you've been rejecting your own feelings until now.

The big problem here is twofold: People are being raised with the messages that emotional pain or discomfort is unacceptable and must be expelled immediately by any means. This belief is what leads to the second issue—choosing self-medicating strategies to try to escape the pain, as opposed to dealing with it.

> Every addiction reaction is a call for an equal
> and opposite loving action.

I've lost close friends to suicide, they would not face their wounds. One was a dear friend who had lived thirty years sober before he ended his life. I'd always worried about him. He attended spirituality seminars and churches with famous, upbeat pastors, and listened to meditation tapes. But I knew that these were only strategies he was using to mask his pain, and he was troubled inside. He could not show his anger or sorrow. I pleaded with him to get help. Sober a long time, he thought he knew what he was doing. He could not see he had transferred his addiction from alcohol and drugs to extreme exercise and spirituality. When his age no longer allowed him to participate in Ironman competitions, and the quotes and affirmations of his spiritual guru no longer generated the endorphins, he crashed.

The last year of his life, he reenacted the role he'd been put in as a child, that of an unloved victim. He quit his well-paying job and desperately ran from person to person looking for a place to stay and asking for financial assistance. Many people loved him, but when they offered him real solutions rather than temporary funds or shelter, he refused the help. He kept saying he knew he needed to address his childhood trauma, but when I found him a place to go for help, he told me it just wasn't quite the "right vibe." Several weeks later, consumed by his wound, he hung himself, leaving all of us who cared about him reeling in sorrow. His unwillingness to face his pain cost him his life.

This didn't have to be his end.

Anyone can find a way out of the maze. Once you are able to give yourself permission to feel and heal, you won't need to escape your feelings anymore. You can learn to embrace your emotions, so you won't need to self-medicate or otherwise self-destruct. Once you perceive your emotions as a valued aid rather than your enemy, you can grant yourself the power to heal.

Self-Evaluation Questionnaire

Identify Your Fears

1. Are you ready to make the commitment to face your pain?
2. What scares you about facing your pain?
3. What are some of the things that cause you to react?
4. If you felt peaceful, without the invisible hole, would you still want to be addicted?

Second Barrier: Release the Pain

Kahlil Gibran wrote that "Your pain is the breaking of the shell that encloses your understanding."[1] I believe this is true, and I've seen it when the addiction can no longer obscure the pain, and it comes spilling out. This outpouring is the beginning of your healing, the cracking of your wall.

When you were young and suffered, you might have learned to close your heart. This action served as a temporary protection against the onslaught of traumatic and painful events. Many of my patients have been able to recall the exact moment they made the decision to emotionally check out. I zoned out at age five when, after an extremely painful moment, I consciously thought, *I don't like it here. I'm never going to feel again.* Throughout my childhood, to protect myself from the cruelty I witnessed and endured, I shut down my heart. It was the only way I knew to temper my suffering.

Shutting down emotionally serves a purpose. It can help a child make it through early life without going insane. Some people dissociate, and when trauma hits, they feel themselves leave their bodies and go through life being observers rather than participants. Regardless of how it happens, once the heart closes, it often stays shut, even when it would be safer for it to remain wide-open.

Keeping pain out also blocks joy. When my heart was closed, I saw the world in black and white. Even though I lived in one of the most beautiful places, I could not see the living color all around. I went through the motions of life without the emotions. Those who loved me did not get to experience the intimacy they naturally wanted to share with me.

As long as your heart remains closed, you cannot heal. You can go through the motions, but you will not get results. If you want to heal, the wall must come down. Pain is unavoidable, but when you allow it to wash right through you, love will follow.

There is no safety in a closed heart. You cannot shut out the pain without keeping out the light. You can't have it both ways—you either go through life like a robot, or you embrace all the sorrow, grief, and broken dreams along with the joy, victories, and fulfilled dreams. With love as your guide, the disappointments will be short-lived and the happiness long.

I like to think of the heart as the emotional recycling center. If your heart is open, you can release your pain, and by the time you're finished crying, your emotions can shift from heavy gloom to uplifting hope.

Many people have sought spirituality without embracing an open heart, and they accomplish nothing. Spirituality is found with an open heart—one that feels, one that forgives, one that can love. If you cannot open your heart to loving yourself and others, you can't expect a fairy godmother to appear, tap you on the head, and make all your dreams come true. Remember, you already have all the love you ever need right inside you, and when you share and receive that love with others, you will have found spirituality. It's through acts of sharing love that you feel love for yourself and others.

Sometimes pain is the thing that forces open the door to our hearts. If you're addicted and you're fortunate, at some point, your pain will become so great, it will crack open the shell that has kept you separated from the love inside you. In this case, pain is a lifesaver. Just as pain in the body tells you something is wrong and needs to be addressed, emotional pain can motivate you to do what you need to do to heal, even if it means getting help. Addressing old pain and trauma alone can be incredibly difficult. If at any point you feel that you need support to help you through the process or if you are starting to think maybe it's not worth it to continue, make sure you contact a therapist. Getting help is a sign of courage, not weakness. Make sure you see someone trained in mental health and addictions who takes into account the important spiritual component of healing.

When something traumatic happens, feeling pain and loss is natural. However, it doesn't have to lead to or feed addiction. When you allow yourself to feel pain and grieve, you will naturally heal. But if you refuse to accept a loss that is final by deluding yourself that it is only temporary or by suppressing the pain of the loss, you will prolong your suffering, guaranteed.

Elisabeth Kübler-Ross, famous for naming the five stages of a grieving process (denial, anger, bargaining, depression, and acceptance), has helped us better understand how we heal from loss. These stages are normal and natural, and if we move through them all, we can recover from even the most painful losses, at least to the point that we become free of the need to go nuclear. The problem occurs when we resist feeling the grief and get stuck in it. Before you can fully recover from addiction, you will need to grieve your unhealed pain.

At first, to deny a traumatic event is normal, as it can provide a buffer from the intensity of the event. It's also natural to try to bargain with a higher power or person: "I'll do anything if you'll stop this from happening." It's only natural to feel angry and depressed because the traumatic event represents a loss of something valued. When you allow yourself to feel these painful emotions, you can release them, and a new door will open to what the future holds. When you feel your emotions and let them go, it's amazing how fast you can heal the pain of the loss. If you have been unable to grieve because you've never learned how, now is the time.

> **If your heart is open, you can release your pain.**

This step is the most important part of your healing process, and it's the most uncomfortable. Many of us have been conditioned by our caretakers to suppress feelings, and we've mastered the ability to shove them down deep. You might dislike feeling vulnerable. You might believe that crying is shameful. You might fear that allowing your emotions to surface and be visible puts an unnecessary burden on others. Many people have told me they are afraid to cry because once they start, they might never stop. Some have told me they don't allow themselves to get angry anymore because they always regret doing so.

Like any wound, if left unattended, it will only get worse. You can ignore it or numb it, but it won't go away. For example, if you had an addicted parent and you felt abandoned because it seemed the person was always absent (literally or emotionally), you most likely have attracted people who also leave you with feelings of abandonment. Whenever you feel abandoned by someone now, you might feel powerless to do anything but react. What you do with your reactions can be empowering or debilitating; it's your choice. You can learn to tend to (love) a reactivated wound, so you can stop living with the effects of childhood pain and suffering (fear) and regain emotional stability.

One of my patients attracted men who came on strong, but as soon as the chase was over, they would abruptly back off, leaving her sad and bewildered. When a guy would withdraw, she would try harder to get him back by calling him or catering to his needs, but her neediness would push him even further away.

Through therapy, she realized that her reactions were a reenactment of her relationship with an alcoholic father, who was loving and attentive when he was drunk but solemn and cold when he was not. She was replaying her wound in an unconscious and misguided attempt to reach back in time and receive consistent love from her father. Even though not all of these men were alcoholics like her father, they were all unstable and emotionally inconsistent, stimulating the same feelings of abandonment.

Once she started sitting with her feelings and began using the exercises described below to heal her pain, her reactions no longer controlled her, no matter how the other person behaved. She was able to recognize that her reactions were about her father, not the person in front of her. And from a place of neutrality she was then able to do whatever was necessary to take care of herself rather than being at the mercy of her unhealed past.

> When you choose love over fear, you are making the decision to purge the pain.

Another patient, who described his mother as irresponsible (always running late, no organization in the home, no structure), found himself reacting to people who showed similar traits. In a fear-based attempt to keep his wound at bay, he micromanaged his employees. Then, whenever an employee's behavior triggered his unconscious memory of his scatter-brained mother (arriving late, having messy offices, being disorganized), he would blow up and yell at them, which caused further disruption and chaos when the flustered employee would quit. Once he allowed himself to feel the pain and learned how to use his reactions as cues that he needed to engage in self-reflection, he regained his self-control. Rather than suffering the effects of his impulsive reactions, he was able to delegate someone else to address the employee imperfections, and his employees were better able to coalesce as a team instead of being squelched by a frustrated authority figure.

Whatever your reasons for holding in your emotions, it's time to give them up. Holding in your pain only drills a deeper hole. When you choose love over fear, you are making the decision to purge the pain and replace it with acceptance and peace. Every time you release another part of the pain, you have taken another step out of the maze.

Pain-Release Exercise

There are two reasons for tears: to cleanse the eyes and to cleanse the heart. If you've trained yourself to hold in sorrow, you've missed out on one of the natural highs you could get freely. Crying produces oxytocin and endorphins, and both are mood enhancers.[2] When you cry, you not only get the benefit of releasing grief but the side benefit of feeling a natural high.

Most people who are addicted don't even realize that every time they experience an intense negative emotional reaction, they have reopened an old wound. And every time a new wound occurs, it's like tossing sticks of dynamite into a smoldering volcano, brewing up the next explosion or "going nuclear." Spewing lava everywhere only burns others and creates intense amounts of regret for having lost control.

Conversely, when the feelings come up and then get shoved back down, the inner battle fuels the vortex of pain and expands the invisible hole. Rather than dealing with painful emotions, the addict reenacts the same childhood message that it's not okay to feel. This is the true cause of relapse—unhealed pain that fuels intense reactions in people who have not been taught how to utilize their emotions in a healthy way.

Here's where you get the opportunity to choose love over fear. It might feel easier to ignore the reaction, to try to get rid of the feelings as quickly as possible, or to be self-righteous by telling yourself your avoidance is "taking the high road." These are all examples of choosing fear, and what I call a spiritual bypass. It never works. Spirituality is not about suppressing emotions. Spiritual fitness means we can convert our negative feelings into love, but we can only do so by feeling them and allowing them to dissipate. You will never get well by ignoring the pain in the vortex or the hollowness of the invisible hole. The decision to face the pain *is* choosing love, and when you choose that, healing happens.

Every time you do it, you are lifting yourself out of the maze a little further. Instead of ignoring the vortex of pain spinning just beneath the surface of your existence, you can claim these feelings and love yourself through them. Be sure that you do this exercise *before* you do anything else to relieve the internal tension. As long as you feed the wound with an addiction, you keep the addiction alive. You might not have had a loving person to help you when you were young, but you can be there for yourself now. In fact, if you want to get better, you *must* be the one that is there for you now.

The technique I am going to describe was taught to me by Michael Singer, when I regularly attended his lectures in Alachua, Florida. For those of you who are interested and would like to know more, Singer wrote *The Untethered Soul.*

The most vital time to use this exercise is when you're aware you're having one of the "nuclear" emotional reactions we spoke of earlier, but you can use this anytime you sense agitation or internal discomfort. No matter what, do this exercise before you turn to drink, drugs, food, sex, or anything else such as inappropriately venting your emotions to get rid of the discomfort.

This is not a one-time action. I recommend that you do the exercise each and every time you feel a reaction. Years of pain that ate away at you, expanding the invisible hole, won't go away in one or two releases. When I first started doing this process, I felt waves of rage and cried buckets of tears, but now my reactions are only a flicker of emotion. There's no right number of times to do this exercise, only each time another part of your wound surfaces to heal. Depending on the amount of trauma, this might require you to do the exercise ten or a hundred or a thousand times. The point is, you do it as a practice, not as a one-shot, "set it and forget it" solution.

First, whenever you notice any *strong emotional reaction that lingers,* no matter what you are doing, go someplace where you can be alone and close your eyes. As soon as possible, remove yourself (even if you have to go into a public bathroom) and do the exercise. (If you are at home, you can download and use the guided meditation found on my website, DrDonnaMarks.com.)

Get still, close your eyes, and place your attention on the area of your body where you feel the disturbance. Focus on the internal reaction you are experiencing. Breathe. Imagine you are watching yourself doing the release exercise and you are safe. Allow all your feelings to surface. Some people rush through the exercise while having a reaction; they close their eyes for a brief time, then nothing happens. The key is to stay in the process until the reaction arises and completely dissipates. You can feel the toxic energy moving and dissipating. Make sure you keep a steady flow of breathing. Holding your breath will block emotions, and the feelings need to come out.

If you stay with this, you may begin to notice memories of abuse or trauma that you've kept deep down are triggered by the current event. These make up part of the pain that has been bottled up inside you for most of your life, and these memories are the roots of your reactions. Allow yourself to feel everything: anger, sadness, fear, or anything else that's going on. Just be with the emotions.

With your eyes closed, keep breathing and stay with your feelings until there is nothing left to feel. When the emotional charge has neutralized and a sense of calm comes over you, open your eyes. Let yourself be quiet for a while, so you can regain your emotional balance.

> **Choosing love over fear does not mean you
> need to be perfect.**

That's all there is to it, a few simple steps that can provide enormous healing. Just be careful that you don't tell yourself this is so easy that you don't need to go through the simple steps every time your reactions warrant it. Here's where many people cheat themselves out of feeling good. They think because they've done this exercise a few times, they're done. Not so. As much as possible, you must do this whenever you notice yourself having an emotional reaction. Otherwise, only partial healing occurs. It's not enough to follow this technique a few times; it is a lifelong tool—whenever you have a strong reaction that you can't shake, practice recognizing it as an opportunity to heal another piece of the past, and do the exercise again. Over time, your reactions will become less frequent and less intense, and will dissipate quicker. If you do this exercise before you engage in old addictive behaviors, you can replace the addiction with peace.

Choosing love over fear does not mean you need to be perfect. The most important thing is that you keep embracing your emotions and doing the exercise. The cure is a process. You might find yourself engaging in old, self-defeating behaviors or even relapsing; this does not mean you are failing. It only means there is more work to do—never give up.

Self-Evaluation Questionnaire

Identify Your Barriers to Releasing Pain

1. If you had been your parent, what would you have done differently?
2. Are you willing to re-parent yourself now? If so, what guidelines would you follow?
3. Do you remember a time when you closed your heart? If so, why?
4. Remember a time when your heart was open. What did that feel like?
5. If your heart is closed, how does that block you from healing your pain?
6. Are you willing to go through a short-term process of letting your heart open, so it can cleanse your pain? Describe what that would look like.
7. Write down any concerns you have about feeling your pain and how you can comfort yourself.

12

STEP TWO TOWARD LOVE—
FORGIVENESS

To err is human, to forgive, divine.

—Alexander Pope

Once you've healed your pain, finding forgives is natural. *A Course in Miracles* tells us, "Forgiveness is the key to happiness."[1] Let that sink in. Without forgiveness, your healing cannot be complete. The ego tells us we are foolish to forgive, but when you've chosen love, holding on to resentments is clearly boring and unproductive. You learn there is no value in keeping a wound alive, and you are much better off feeling the pain, releasing it, and letting go of the anger and resentment. Whatever the cause of your pain—loss of a loved one, loss of pride, financial loss—it doesn't matter; it's all the same. To heal, we must forgive.

A Course in Miracles teaches us to change our perception and the result is the miracle of healing our pain through love. People who heal their pain can change their perception of childhood abuse from anger and hurt to compassion and forgiveness. They begin to see that the person who hurt them was sick. When we forgive, resentment is replaced with compassion.

Forgiveness allows us to stop dragging around the heavy load of long-ago events. Hanging on to old baggage would be like writing a giant book about every bad memory of your life, then lugging it around wherever you went. It would always be there, slowing you down, tiring you out. You'd drag it out of bed with you in the morning and into bed with you at night. You'd work, dance, and make love with a hundred-pound book strapped to you at all times. Not much fun. Now that your wound is healing, you can finish each chapter and put it on a shelf called "My Life." You no longer carry the heavy load around, yet the stories will remain an important part of who you are—just not what you are.

When new reactions emerge, your practice is to continue to purge your charged emotions—feel your pain and release it, and also let go of those bad stories one at a time. Every time a part of the wound heals, the load is a little lighter, and life gets easier. One morning you wake up without any baggage at all, able to feel lighthearted and look forward to the day—full of happiness.

One of my favorite teachings in *A Course in Miracles* is that there are no sins, only mistakes.[2] Mistakes are part of being human, and "all things are lessons God would have you learn."[3] Now that you've come this far, remember that it's only natural you will make mistakes along the way. Give yourself permission to be human. When you make mistakes, use them to learn, so you can grow from them rather than staying stuck in guilt and shame.

When patients relapse, they tell me how awful they feel. My intent is that they don't waste precious time and energy beating themselves up, so I encourage them to explore what happened prior to the relapse. Most of the time such replapses were triggered by an emotional reaction. I remind these patients that this is an opportunity to dig deep to locate the unresolved pain that caused the reaction and release it, so they aren't triggered again.

When you give yourself permission to make mistakes, and you make the effort to understand what caused you to make the mistake, you can pave the way to make a more loving choice next time. Generally, any mistake you make will do far less damage than the reaction to the mistake if you beat yourself up. Don't let mistakes get you down; hold your head up high and choose love rather than relapse when you're tempted to castigate yourself or numb out.

When you stumble, remember to reach out for support from people who can help you, especially from someone who's been where you are and knows what you're going through. Another way to love yourself through your mistakes is to talk to yourself as if you were a young person who just screwed up. Rather than shaming that little person, you could say something like, "It's okay to make mistakes. I'm not mad at you. I don't expect you to be perfect, and I love you no matter what. We can talk about what happened, then you can do better next time."

Resentment Release Exercise

It's not always easy to forgive someone who caused you great harm, but it is in your best interests to do so. When your invisible hole is carrying the residue of resentment, your healing is not complete. When you make the choice to love yourself, there's no room for resentments; love cannot live where resentments reside.

Part of loving yourself is remaining free of toxic thoughts and feelings. Some people think that keeping up a wall offers protection from further hurt or betrayal, but this is not true. Resentments only maintain barriers that keep you in the maze, just as the unhealthy ego wants.

I'm not suggesting that we excuse unacceptable behavior, but rather, as *A Course in Miracles* suggests, to look at it differently. There's no freedom in blaming people who were not well enough to provide a healthy template. Most abusers were abused as children and are too sick or ashamed to learn a better way. Maybe someday more parents will take classes that teach good parenting skills. Meanwhile, for those of us who were abused or became perpetrators ourselves, our greatest hope of change is through healing our painful past and forgiveness. When we forgive, we lift the veil of shame and allow ourselves to open up to permanent healing.

> **When you make the choice to love yourself, there's no room for resentments.**

One of the most important concepts *A Course in Miracles* offers is that self-condemnation is underneath every unforgiven thought toward someone else. At first I could not wrap my mind around it. It seemed so ridiculous. I wondered how a little child could feel responsible for being abused. But then I thought back to my own childhood, and I remembered thinking, *What did I do to cause him to hurt me?* Only five years old and emotionally crushed by a stepfather I loved, it had to be my fault that such raging hatred was cast upon me. Later, when healing my emotional wounds, I better understood *A Course in Miracles*. I blamed myself, and I had taken over the role of beating myself up when no one else was.

In addition to the Pain Release exercise, you can employ other ways to purge toxic feelings so you can reach forgiveness. One effective technique is to write out the thoughts and feelings that are disturbing you. This is a healthy way to vent toxic energy without lashing out at someone and harming a relationship. Once you diffuse the negative energy, you can be more open to having a rational conversation that will hopefully lead to a more loving understanding. I don't recommend typing your feelings out on your computer. Once someone accidentally copied me on a letter intended for someone else that was full of unpleasantries about me. I forgave her. God does have a sense of humor.

Another technique that I learned and highly recommend to achieve forgiveness is to write a goodbye letter to someone with whom you have unfinished business. Again, this is not for the purpose of sending it to anyone, as it is to give you closure by releasing the pain of unresolved grief. Also, this exercise is equally effective whether the person is alive or not. In the letter, you can recall the good and the bad, how you felt about that person, and the effect they had on you. This is the opportunity to let it all hang out, so don't hold back. Take your time and make a point of getting into as many memories as possible. Make sure you allow all anger, sorrow, remorse, and any other pain to come out. When all your memories have been purged, end your letter by saying goodbye. Make sure you say everything you ever wished you would have, including, "I forgive you" or "I'm sorry." Let them know you needed to do this so you could have closure. When you have nothing else to say, you can tuck the letter away someplace safe, shred it, or find a safe way to burn it as a ceremonial goodbye.

> **By letting go, you can release old pain and set yourself free to enjoy a new future.**

Florence did not want to write a letter to her deceased dad, but she finally mustered up the courage and did so. When she read it to me, I was brought to tears. She told her dad that she was hurt and angry that he had been physically and sexually abusive toward her as a child. She wrote down a few examples and, as she read, grew angry. She kept repeating, "I can't understand. Why did you do this to me? It's ruined my life." Florence pounded the pillow next to her and kept asking, "Why?" Then, suddenly, she grew quiet. The tears poured out, and she whimpered like a little girl. Finally, after an exhausting catharsis, she said, "I get it. He was a sick man. I remember one time he told me that he was frequently taken to the barn and beaten when he was a boy. His mother hung on to him like he was the man of the house. He couldn't wait to get out of the house and enlisted in the military when he was only eighteen. He drank away his pain. It ultimately killed him. I wish he'd gotten help instead of hurting me. But it must have been hell to be in his body." Florence's letter brought closure to the unfinished business with her dad and allowed her to move beyond the pain locked inside her.

You can write to every person with whom you are holding on to unresolved grief. By letting go, you can release old pain and set yourself free to enjoy a new future. Once you have purged the pain associated with your memories of that person, you can see them in a new light, with a lens unclouded by the past.

As adults, we can notice how, beneath our grievances, there are always feelings of inadequacy. "I should have been smarter," "I shouldn't have trusted him or her," and "I should have listened to my gut" are typical comments that accompany resentment. We cannot expect ourselves to be perfect; it's easy to trust the wrong people, and everyone makes mistakes.

One patient, Herman, was a recovering alcoholic and addict, who, while in a workshop I was teaching, uncovered the root of his addiction. Herman had never shared his secret with anyone, but he unveiled the trauma that led to his addiction. When he was about six years old, Herman's parents had left him with his two-year-old brother at a fountain while they went to the restroom. When they returned, Herman was sitting on the side of the fountain daydreaming. When his parents asked him where his little brother was, he realized he'd forgotten all about him. Tragically, his little brother had fallen in the fountain and drowned.

Herman's parents blamed him for his brother's death, causing him to feel ashamed. Herman also blamed himself for his brother's drowning, and he used alcohol and drugs to escape the pain he felt. His life had become a long ordeal of silent suffering. The compassion of the other members helped him release years of pent-up pain through gut-wrenching sobs and wails. But the real miracle occurred when, for the first time, Herman was able to see that it was not him who was at fault, but his parents who'd made the mistake of leaving an infant in the care of another child. Herman was then able to free himself from blame and understand that his parents had paid dearly for their own poor judgment, and no one needed to bear the cross of human failure any longer.

> When you have forgiven yourself and others and let
> love in, that love will replace your need for addiction.

A Course in Miracles teaches us that we are not sinners; we are merely human beings, and we all make mistakes. Rather than condemn ourselves, we need to simply acknowledge our "errors" and do what we can to correct them. But the unhealthy ego uses guilt to keep us in a state of feeling unworthy. As we discussed earlier, guilt rarely stops us from doing something we are intent on doing—especially an addictive behavior. Remember, guilt and anger only cover up our fears and lead us to believe we won't be happy without our pseudo-comfort. But the addiction provides only short-term relief for long-term misery, and it reinjures us. The invisible hole is never filled, and the suffering continues.

If you want out of the maze, you must find and fill the invisible hole with love and positive esteem for yourself. When you have forgiven yourself and others and let love in, that love will replace your need for addiction. You will no longer need an external fix for something that is readily available within.

You will no longer need to substitute an addiction for love because your choosing love is the cure.

Self-Evaluation Questionnaire

Identify Your Blocks to Forgiveness

1. Do you hold resentments toward someone else that you haven't been able to shake off?
2. How have those resentments benefited you?
3. Make a list of everyone you haven't forgiven and why.

4. Looking at each situation, write down how you might have blamed yourself.
5. Write a letter to each person, including yourself. Expel all of your pain and anger, then either shred the letter or safely burn it, letting it all go.
6. Write a letter to yourself as though you were a loving parent, forgiving yourself for being less than perfect. Remind yourself you are human, and that humans make mistakes. Tell yourself that you are loved and that the more you learn to love yourself, the more loved you will feel.

STEP THREE TOWARD LOVE—REPLACE ADDICTION WITH LOVING BEHAVIORS

Yet the ego, through encouraging the search for love very actively, makes one proviso; do not find it.

—*A Course in Miracles*

N ow that your wall is crumbling down and you're letting love in, you're ready for the final step of self-love: replacing the addiction with new, fulfilling actions. Remember, every addiction is a substitute for love, so to forget about your addiction, you must replace every addiction with an act of love.

I want you to visualize yourself as healthy, healed, and out of the maze of addiction. Take some time to picture your ideal life free from addiction. How do you see yourself living? What experiences will you have? Will you wake up feeling excited about the day? Will your life have added meaning and a sense of purpose? Would you be engaged in helping others? Would you enjoy time alone, more time with friends, a mixture of both? What hobbies would you be loving? Would you have a romantic relationship that felt safe and enriching to both people? What would your home look like decorated in your own personal taste? Would you have any new pets? A garden? What would you be doing for fun? What lifelong dreams would you be fulfilling? How will you handle disappointment, setbacks, and loss? This last is one of the most important questions. The way you learn to handle life's bumps can say more about your healing than how you handle the times when things are going great.

Now that you have a picture of your ideal life, write it down. For example, here's Jack's ideal life:

- I'll stay sober and avoid places and situations where
  I used to relapse.
- I'll get to see my kids again. It's been three years, but
  the reunification therapy has worked, and I've earned back
  their trust.
- I'm out of debt and enjoying my career.
- I'm comfortable being alone because I have a couple of
  new hobbies that keep me busy.
- I'm enjoying self-help books and growing.
- I go to sleep peacefully and wake up happy.
- I'm exercising and getting in shape.
- I stopped eating sugar and lost twenty pounds.
- When I need company, I have new sober friends with
  whom to socialize and attend meetings.
- I find a cause I believe in and volunteer.
- Eventually, I meet someone who's also into personal growth.

> **The way you learn to handle life's bumps can say
> more about your healing than how you handle the
> times when things are going great.**

Next, create a list of things you like to do or have always wanted to learn how to do. Here's some of Jack's list:

- Take cooking lessons
- Learn how to play bridge
- Take scuba lessons
- Go on a spiritual retreat in Peru
- Visit the Louvre Museum

Lastly, promptly banish all thoughts of relapsing with an immediate new behavior.

I will give you a few examples here, but you will be best served by developing your own interventions. Whenever you even think about the addiction, you need to take action right then. You don't want to wait until you've thought about it so much that you find yourself relapsing before you ever realize what happened. The minute you have that fleeting thought cross your mind, you immediately do the loving behavior.

Here are common triggers that precede relapse:

Loneliness

- Reach out to someone. Promptly get on the phone and call a support person.
- Get to a recovery meeting.
- Go online and join an organization that interests you.
- Do volunteer work.
- Find someone who needs a ride to a meeting, the store, or the doctor and take them regularly.
- Join a walking/jogging group.

Anger

- Talk it out with a trusted support person or therapist.
- Journal your feelings.
- Eat a healthy meal (in case your blood sugar is low).
- Do the healing/feeling exercises outlined in the previous section. (Face the pain, release the pain.)
- Write a letter, but don't send it.
- Pound some pillows.

Sadness/Depression

- Same as the first four items for anger.
- Watch a sad movie—it helps you cry and get the pain out.
- Read a self-help book on grieving.
- Join a bereavement group.
- Write down things you can control and things you can't.
- Make a list of everything for which you feel grateful.
- Go to extra recovery meetings.

Anxiousness

- Close your eyes, take three deep breaths, sit with the feelings.
- Identify the fear underneath the anxiety.
- Write down a solution to the fear.
- Pray.
- Put a plan into place.

Overwhelm

- Rest.
- Make a to-do list and cross off one item at a time.
- Take a break—have a cup of tea, take a ten-minute walk on the beach, listen to a meditation recording.
- Ask for help.
- Permit yourself to say no.
- Remind yourself you always get through stressful times.

Resentfulness

- Write down what happened and why you're resentful.
- Write down anything about the situation that you blame yourself for.
- Do the anger work (above).
- Pray for the willingness to forgive.

One patient who'd gone through this three-step process and had suffered a great deal of pain after a divorce described his exit from the maze. "A few weeks ago, I was stuck in my apartment alone during a storm. I could have called someone. I didn't; instead I decided to do what I've learned: face the pain and feel it. The pain crept over me, like a dark ghost, telling me all kinds of things: you're a loser; what the hell is the matter with you? I remembered hearing that same question throughout my childhood. I sat with the feelings of failure as each day grew darker. I was alone—so alone. I wanted to call my ex. I didn't. It felt like I was falling in a hole, and I let it consume me. The next morning, I looked out of the window and saw the sky. I heard the waves and the sounds of seagulls; I smelled the smell of coffee brewing. I wasn't alone anymore. I was here, with myself, and beauty was all around me. Family photos, a nice home, my favorite books, a file on the desk full of lifetime awards, art, *A Course in Miracles* book beside me. I now have the peace I'd never felt before. I love my life. I'm glad I didn't give up; it's been a difficult process, and there was so much to release, to heal. I'm grateful for the marriage and the divorce; they brought up the deeper wounds I never had the courage to face. Had I not been addicted to her, I would have kept old trauma safely at bay, along with all the love I feel, including the compassion I feel for her, which has replaced the anger and resentment. Someday, I will meet someone. Right now, I'm on a different journey of loving myself and the world around me."

You, too, can find the peace you were intended to have. You can save yourself years of "searching but never finding." A child in pain has few choices. It's not possible for children to leave an abusive or neglectful home without risking death in the outside world, though in some cases they might be safer out there than at home. But now that you are no longer a child, you can choose to make your own rules—you get to choose love over fear. Answering the following questions can help you identify areas of your life where you have not forgiven, so you can begin to forgive the people and events that precipitated your original pain. Once you forgive, you are out of the maze. To stay out, you will have to keep letting go and choosing love.

> You, too, can find the peace you were intended to have.

14

EXIT THE MAZE FOR GOOD

The only real prison is fear, and the only real freedom
is freedom from fear.

—Aung San Suu Kyi

You've exited the maze; now let's talk about some strategies for continuing your self-care so that you remain cured. Life is not perfect. It has its ups and downs. And if you stay addiction free, you can learn how to grow with the imperfections in yourself and others. If you remember to choose love rather than harm, you will be able to sustain the happiness that replaces any need for self-destructive addiction—even when you screw up.

More Ways to Love Yourself

You are the most important person you will ever love. If you've been addicted, we can safely assume that you're been trying to find love in all the wrong ways to make up for any sense of deficiency. When you give up "something you love" and replace it with an act of love, this is where real freedom lies.

Giving up something, even if it's not good for you, must be replaced with something that is good for you. Think of filling the invisible hole as a daily practice of self-love and self-care, not too much or too little. Love is all around you. Love will not intrude upon you or force its way through your walls. If you want the solution, you have to let it in.

Remember that the cure is an ongoing process. You always have the freedom to choose love over addiction. You are retraining your brain to replace self-destructive acts with acts of love. Every time you choose to treat yourself with love, you are rebuilding self-trust. It feels awful to be told that you're loved, then get treated like crap, so be sure that as you pledge your love to yourself, you treat yourself well.

Care for Your Time

Every moment of every day is a gift. Joy and happiness are natural; you do not have to waste time pursuing them. You are here for a reason; give your life the chance it deserves; it awaits you. There are two doors: one says LOVE, one says FEAR; one leads to heaven, the other to hell. It's up to you. I suspect if you've read this far, whether you realize it or not, you've made the decision for love. *A Course in Miracles* states: "Love waits on welcome, not on time."[1] This moment is as important as any other; your dreams await you. Grasp your lifelong vision for your life; you know what it is, so let it unfold. It's very easy—one addiction, one solution, and one path to freedom. The sooner you open your heart, the sooner your life will bloom.

Care for Your Body

Care for your body as if you were caring for a young child. In addition to the things we outlined in the section on healthy parenting, you can do more. This means that you eat to live, not live to eat. Instead of going for fast food, go for good food. Avoid putting toxins in your body and toxic people in your brain.

> **Prepare for success, lay out a plan, then wait for its arrival. Many plans derail when they are forced to happen too soon.**

Give your body the exercise it needs to stay fit but without fixating on having a perfect body—another invisible hole that has no end. Take the time for pampering, but to feel good on the inside, not just to look good on the outside. During times of stress, you can double down on all of these strategies.

Make friends with people who have your back, not who will put a knife in your back. Prepare for success, lay out a plan, then wait for its arrival. Many plans derail when they are forced to happen too soon.

Care for Your Spirit

Listen to yourself and trust your spirit, your internal navigation system. Take time to commune with beauty—sunsets, the sounds of nature, walks in the fresh air, beautiful music—and ground yourself in your responsibilities. Deeply inhale the scent of roses and all the perfume of nature. Spend time in solitude to listen to your higher consciousness while you keep both feet firmly planted on the ground.

Allow yourself to be fascinated with everything around you. Life keeps regenerating itself, and every single thing you see—your clothes, computers, dishes, furniture, jewelry, windows—came out of the ground. Imagine that. All creation has made our lives easier. We don't know what it would be like to live in caves and fend off wild animals for food; we take so much for granted. Gratitude is the circuitry that will keep you plugged into this creative life force.

All the love you want and need is right inside of you, and your commitment to that inward journey is what will keep you out of the maze forever.

Care for Your Relationships

Allowing people to love you is an important part of self-love. We are not supposed to be isolated; we are designed to share and receive love with others. *A Course in Miracles* teaches that sharing and receiving are the same. The loving relationships you develop offer opportunities to share and receive love and add fulfillment and satisfaction to life. Many people have been so hurt that they are afraid to trust anyone. If that's how you feel, you can start to realize that you are the most important person you will ever trust. As long as you forgive and keep an open heart, you can overcome any amount of pain. Going forward, if you will listen to your deeper consciousness, your "Holy Spirit," and trust it, you won't get hurt as much because you will receive the protective suggestions offered to you. If bad things do happen, you can use the tools you now have to work through the pain without self-destructing. When you nurture yourself through the grief, you will learn to trust that you can heal no matter what.

> Allowing people to love you is an important part of self-love. We are not supposed to be isolated; we are designed to share and receive love with others.

When you come from love, you can practice balancing your wants and needs with those of others, and by negotiating those mutual needs, you can build sustainable relationships. I call this the "We Program," as opposed to the "Me Program." Instead of being afraid of losing someone if you express your own desires, you share your authentic self. At the same time, you put your loving actions to your words by caring about the other person's wants and needs as much as your own. This doesn't mean we accommodate each other 100 percent of the time, but it means we do the best we can to show we care.

Care for Your Mind

Pause a moment when you're agitated, and act when you are calm. There's no shame in getting help if you need it, but you don't have to entrust your mind to just anyone or any facility. Make sure the people who help you are compassionate and competent. Like any relationship, be choosy and make sure it's a good fit.

Listen to your intuitive mind and allow yourself to develop trust with that part of you. Treasure your memories. Allow the good memories to bloom, and allow the weeds of sorrow to wilt and die.

Allow your mind to be open but wise. If something sounds good but doesn't feel right, make sure the two are aligned before you go forward. Be aware of the ego, the part of the mind that is always waiting to steer you off course. If this happens, you will feel uneasy, but at any time, you can reconnect to the voice of the Holy Spirit.

When Fear Arises

It's only natural that fear will creep into your mind. Remember to repeat the aforementioned exercises—sit with it, identify the fear, come up with solutions. When you feel empty or restless, it's time for a break to give yourself the healthy nurturing and attention you need. Whether you cuddle with a blanket and pillow, fix yourself a cup of hot tea or your favorite (healthy) meal, talk to a loved one, engage in your favorite hobby, listen to music, meditate or commune with your Holy Spirit, or just sit and be, you can do these things to refill your tank with love.

You also can use affirmations. One of my favorites is *I have all the love I need, I am healing, I am not alone, and I have many good things in my life now.* Another favorite is *I'm uncomfortable, but I'm growing fast. All of these feelings are good, even if I don't like them.* The key to using affirmations effectively is to try to feel them deep in your heart and not just say the words. Love is always there for you to call upon. Like anything else, the more you practice choosing love over fear, the better off you are. Whenever you are not at peace, embrace the discomfort and call on love to help you. The answers will come, and they will feel right.

The Goodbye Letter

When you're ready to replace addiction with self-love, it's time to write a goodbye letter to the addiction. It could go like this

> *Dear (fill in the blank),*
> *I need to tell you goodbye. I've tried to make this work, but it's only caused emotional, physical, and spiritual harm. I'm scared to let go, but I know I will be happier without you. I'm going to replace you with things that are good for me. I can see that by staying stuck to you, I've been in a confusing, unhealthy relationship with you. I'm not confused anymore. I'm going to learn how to love myself.*
> *Goodbye.*

After you write the letter, get quiet and let yourself feel whatever emotions arise.

The Hearts Exercise

I'm going to share with you an exercise people in my workshops enjoy doing; it can be a metaphor for how to fill the invisible hole. Even men in their fifties and older who thought this exercise was silly received great joy when they followed the steps.

Buy yourself a good-size clear glass jar and a pad of red construction paper and a pad of black. Cut a few pieces of the black paper into strips and wad them up. Put all of them in the jar. Cut hearts out of the red construction paper. Every time you do something good for yourself, such as walk away from a temptation, embrace your feelings, help someone, take a hot bath, make a good decision, or any other loving act, take out a black wad and put in a red heart. After a while, you will be amazed how your red hearts have replaced the black strips. This can be an ongoing visual reminder of how much you are changing through learning to love yourself.

Cocreate Your Future

Do a vision board. Get a pile of magazines and cut out words and pictures that you want to have manifested in your life. Where do you live? What does your home look like inside and out? Do you have a pet? What kind of toys do you have? Who are you with? What kind of car do you have? How much money have you saved? What is bringing you the most joy? What beauty surrounds you?

Cherish Your Inner Newborn

One last exercise: If you have a picture of when you were a baby, pull it out; if not, you can go ahead without one. I invite you to go back to your birth and have an imaginary conversation with that newborn baby, you. You just left a warm, safe place to come somewhere strange and foreign. Look at how precious you are, how innocent, vulnerable, and dependent on the world around you. You know nothing about rules and regulations; the only need you have right now is to be cared for and loved.

Look deeply into that baby's eyes and show them the love that you have. Tell that baby how happy you are with their arrival and how you will take good care of them now. Hold the baby in your arms, keeping them warm, safe, and secure. Kiss the soft, downy head and send it all the love you've ever felt. Let the baby know you are always here. You are in charge now and can be trusted. You are listening, you care, you will do your best, and when you fall short, you will do better next time. Tell the baby how much you love them and feel the joy of new life, feel the connection to that newborn you. Never let go. Carry that little one in your heart forever.

> **Every time you choose love, you are choosing the gift of life now.**

Every time you choose love, you are choosing the gift of life now, and in that choice, love will continue to bloom. Love is in you and all around you. Love is the only answer; love is the only cure.

Self-Evaluation Questionnaire

Identify Ways that You Feel Loved

1. The following questions are designed to help you come up with your own ideas for ways to love yourself.
2. When you were little, what made you feel loved? Which actions were healthy? For example, hugs, compliments, time together, walks in nature, listening to your feelings? Which actions were unhealthy? For example, being fed pasta or dessert every time you were upset, telling you to get even, being given a cliché to make you feel better but disavowing your pain, and so forth.
3. Which of those actions do you still do that make you feel loved now?
4. List some new ways you can show love to yourself.
5. Is anything stopping you from creating a new healthy template? Describe it.
6. If you had a healthy template now, what would that look like?
7. How would you compare love with spirituality?
   a. Write down three affirmations to use when you're tempted to do unloving things.

b. Write down a gratitude list you can read when you feel a sense of lack.

c. Make a list of people who are safe support for you.

d. Review the exercise on feeling and releasing pain. Write down the steps.

e. Write down three positive things you will do when you make a mistake.

f. Describe how you keep yourself free from pain and in the place of love.

EPILOGUE

LOVE AWAITS

I was once on a spiritual retreat in Peru, and while visiting a village adjacent to a mountainous hiking trail, two of us decided to hike. The trail had many switchbacks, but some were faint and overlapping, and it was easy to become confused as to which path to use. At one point, I was separated from my partner and became completely disorientated. At first, I wasn't worried, but after an hour of aimlessly wandering around, I could hear a haunting voice in my head whispering about every type of imaginary disaster: my group leaving without me, getting snakebit, becoming forever lost. At one point, I could see my way to the base of the mountain, but it wasn't where I'd entered, so I kept going back and forth, getting nowhere. Now two hours had gone by, and my bus would be ready to leave soon, so I pushed through the fear, decided to take my chances, and headed to the base of the mountain. As I got close, a Peruvian man approached and reached up to take my hand. Taking a stranger's hand terrified me, and once again, the voice howled on about people who get kidnapped. Something inside of me pushed past their worried whispers and took the man's hand. Within minutes he'd walked me to my destination. I was so focused on reuniting with my group that I didn't realize he'd left my side before I could thank him. I asked if anyone knew who he was, and they all said they didn't see anyone.

Years later, as I contemplated this event, I realized how it paralleled my greater journey. The mountain was a maze, and somehow, I got lost and was without anyone to guide me out. After losing my friend, I continued my journey, maintaining my self-reliance, which only took me deeper in the maze. At some point, I either had to keep wandering and increase my chances of encountering danger or face the fear of going into the unknown and accepting the help of someone I did not know. That someone magically appeared and disappeared, but they brought me back to my group and safety.

My addictions had me aimlessly wandering through danger while taking me further away from my purpose. I was scared to get out of the maze because of a fear of the unknown. I was afraid to take the hand reaching out to me because of my unwillingness to trust. But once I refused to listen to the voice of fear and accepted the hand of an angel, I was guided back to my fellow humans and safety.

So many of us get bogged down in the mirages of life, and we miss the reasons we are here—to share and receive love. As you go forward, my wish is that you experience the miraculous change in perception: that there is little to fear and much to love. When you look at life through the eyes of love, love will shine back at you. When you choose love, it is impossible to treat yourself in a way that is harmful. When you choose love, you forgive your mistakes and lovingly correct them.

I would like to offer you one final challenge. For one month, follow the steps outlined in this book and see if you improve. You can always go back to the old way, but I suspect that once you get a taste of real love for yourself, the attraction for poor substitutes will lose its appeal.

You never have to be imprisoned in the hell maze again. You won't have to worry about trying to control anything because if you have to control it, it's not good for you, and you don't want it. When you are free, you can be happy no matter what is going on because you know how to love yourself and others through any conflict or problem. After you have been in the maze of addiction and then healed the invisible hole, that hole will fill with light and guide you to all the love you could ever want. Even in your darkest times, if you go within to find even an inkling of that love, you will have recaptured a spark of your birthright for a happy, joyous life. Once that happens, the thought of putting yourself back in addiction prison will lose all of its appeal—not because you are afraid of addiction but because it feels so much better to love yourself and enjoy your life than to tolerate harming your body or bogging down your mind with all the yucky feelings that follow relapse.

If you have chosen to exit the maze, you have already chosen the one solution, and you are on the path to freedom. Love is in you. You can enjoy the journey to find it. There is no better destination. All you have ever wanted and needed has been with you your entire life, right inside your very own heart. Go there now. Love awaits.

ACKNOWLEDGMENTS

I would like to thank my editor, Robin Colucci, for instilling confidence in me that this book could be written and for her exceptional editing skills. To my late psychoanalyst, Donna Bentolilla, who guided me in my journey to healthier relationships. To all my friends in recovery who've been there for me in my darkest hours. To all my family members who are committed to growing together and leading a better way for future generations. To my husband, Skip, for giving me all the space I've needed to fulfill my life purpose in helping people to exit the maze of addiction and reclaim love. To the God of my understanding, Love. When I was ready, the path that was always there opened to me.

APPENDIX

Five-Minute Self-Evaluation:
Addiction Questionnaire

Check any that apply to you *in regard to any behavior*, no matter what it is:

_____ Sometimes I wonder if I have an addiction problem.

_____ I'm baffled that sometimes it's easy to stop and other times I can't.

_____ I've frequently used my willpower to stop doing something, but I go back to doing it again.

_____ I had a parent who was addicted.

_____ I've had a DUI.

_____ I'm afraid if I don't stop, I'm going to lose someone I love.

_____ When I've stopped and then started again, I can feel the disappointment from those who love me.

_____ Part of me wants to quit; part of me tells me I have it under control.

_____ If I didn't do this behavior, things would be better.

_____ I've been arrested, but it hasn't stopped me.

_____ If I had the money I've spent on my habit, I would be financially secure.

_____ I often have a feeling of doom and gloom but don't know why.

_____ I wish I'd never started doing this; it's caused more harm than good.

_____ I live with the fear that something bad will happen if I keep doing this.

_____ I don't understand why I keep doing this behavior.

_____ My habit has caused me problems at work.

_____ I tell myself I don't feel guilty and that I deserve this, but down deep, I do feel bad.

_____ When I have stopped, it feels like something is missing, and I get bored.

_____ I feel there's an emptiness in me that temporarily disappears when I engage in this behavior.

_____ After a period of abstinence, I feel my mind start to dwell on that behavior again.

_____ My children are disappointed when I do this particular thing.

_____ Part of me always talks myself into doing this particular behavior, and then I feel bad after.

_____ I've spent many years on the roller coaster of trying to control this behavior.

_____ I've had health problems because of this behavior.

_____ I've had family problems because of this behavior.

_____ I don't know what's wrong with my emotions; I'm either shut down or gushy.

_____ I've had work problems because of this behavior.

_____ I find myself switching from one habit to the next.

_____ I've spent too much money on this behavior.

_____ My life would be quite different if I'd never started this behavior.

_____ If I didn't do this behavior, I'd feel better about myself.

_____ I've given up on ever being able to stop.

All of these are warning signs of addiction, and any are a red flag to get help.

NOTES

Introduction

1. "Anxiety Disorders," National Alliance on Mental Illness, accessed March 12, 2022, https://www.nami.org/About-Mental-Illness/Mental-Health-Conditions /Anxiety-Disorders#:~:text=Over%2040%20million%20adults%20in,issues%20 with%20anxiety%20each%20year.
2. "Depression," Fact sheet, World Health Organization, accessed September 13, 2021, https://www.who.int/news-room/fact-sheets/detail/depression.
3. Anjel Vahratian et al., "Symptoms of Anxiety or Depressive Disorder and Use of Mental Health Care among Adults During the COVID-19 Pandemic—United States, August 2020–February 2021," Centers for Disease Control and Prevention, *Morbidity and Mortality Weekly Report (MMWR)* 70, no. 13, (April 2, 2021): 490–94, https://www.cdc.gov/mmwr/volumes/70/wr/mm7013e2.htm.
4. Benedict Carey and Robert Gebeloff, "Many People Taking Antidepressants Discover They Can't Quit," *New York Times*, April 7, 2018, https://www.nytimes .com/2018/04/07/health/antidepressants-withdrawal-prozac-cymbalta.html.
5. Julia Robinson, "Antidepressant Prescribing Up 6% in Last Three Months of 2020," *The Pharmaceutical Journal*, March 8, 2021, https://pharmaceutical-journal.com /article/news/antidepressant-prescribing-up-6-since-2019.
6. "Going Off Antidepressants," Harvard Medical School, May 15, 2022, https:// www.health.harvard.edu/diseases-and-conditions/going-off-antidepressants.
7. "Leading Causes of Death," Centers for Disease Control and Prevention, National Center for Health Statistics, page last reviewed January 13, 2022, https://www.cdc .gov/nchs/fastats/leading-causes-of-death.htm/2022.
8. "Preventing Noncommunicable Diseases," World Health Organization, accessed July 5, 2022, https://www.who.int/activities/preventing-noncommunicable-diseases.
9. "Noncommunicable Diseases," Pan American Health Organization, accessed May 21, 2022, https://www.paho.org/en/topics/noncommunicable-diseases; "Heart Disease Facts," Center for Disease Control and Prevention, accessed May 22, 2022, https://www.cdc.gov/heartdisease/facts.htm; "Fresh Look at Cancer Shows Smoking, Obesity Top Causes," NBC News, accessed May 22, 2022, https://www .nbcnews.com/health/cancer/fresh-look-cancer-shows-smoking-obesity-top -causes-n822836; "Type 2 Diabetes Causes and Risk Factors," WebMD, May 16, 2021, https://www.webmd.com/diabetes/diabetes-causes#:~:text=Although%20 not%20everyone%20with%20type,cases%20in%20the%20United%20States;

"Stroke," Mayo Clinic, accessed May 21, 2022, https://www.mayoclinic.org
/diseases-conditions/stroke/symptoms-causes/syc-20350113#:~:text=There%20
are%20two%20main%20causes,doesn't%20cause%20lasting%20symptoms.

10. "Alcohol Facts and Statistics," National Institute on Alcohol Abuse and Alcoholism,
updated March 2022, https://www.niaaa.nih.gov/publications/brochures-and-fact
-sheets/alcohol-facts-and-statistics.

11. "Drug Abuse Statistics," National Center for Drug Abuse Statistics, accessed May
19, 2020, https://drugabusestatistics.org.

12. "Statistics of Gambling Addiction 2016," North American Foundation for
Gambling Addiction Help, accessed March 15, 2022, https://nafgah.org
/statistics-gambling-addiction-2016/.

13. Neal L. Benowitz, "Nicotine Addiction," *The New England Journal of Medicine*
362, no. 24 (2010): 2295-2303, https://doi.org/10.1056/nejmra0809890.

14. Michael Candelaria, "Food Addiction Numbers Rising," *Orlando Sentinel*,
September 2, 2016, www.orlandosentinel.com/health/os-food-addiction-numbers
-rising-20160902-story.html.

15. Nadine DeNinno, "Sex Addiction Epidemic: Study Finds 9 Million Americans Are
Sex Addicts," *International Business Times*, November 30, 2011, www.ibtimes.com
/sex-addiction-epidemic-study-finds-9-million-americans-are-sex-addicts-376908.

16. Mara Tyler, "Shopping Addiction," Healthline, updated August 29, 2016, https://
www.healthline.com/health/addiction/shopping.

17. "Drug Abuse Statistics," National Center for Drug Abuse Statistics, accessed May 19,
2020, https://drugabusestatistics.org.

Chapter 1

1. NIDA, "Is Drug Addiction Treatment Worth Its Cost?" National Institute on
Drug Abuse, June 3, 2020, https://nida.nih.gov/publications/principles-drug
-addiction-treatment-research-based-guide-third-edition/frequently-asked
-questions/drug-addiction-treatment-worth-its-cost.

2. NIDA, "Costs of Substance Abuse," National Institute on Drug Abuse, updated
April 2017, https://archives.drugabuse.gov/trends-statistics/costs-substance-abuse.

3. Patti Verbanas, "Are You Addicted to Technology?," *Rutgers Today*, Rutgers University, October 7, 2021, https://www.rutgers.edu/news/are-you-addicted-technology.

4. Serge H. Ahmed, Karine Guillem, and Youna Vandaele, "Sugar Addiction:
Pushing the Drug-Sugar Analogy to the Limit," *Current Opinion in Clinical Nutrition and Metabolic Care* 16, no. 4 (July 2013), https://doi.org/10.1097/mco
.0b013e328361c8b8.

5. *Alcoholics Anonymous Big Book*, 4th ed. (New York: Alcoholics Anonymous World
Services, 2001), 30.

6. *Merriam-Webster*, s.v. "insanity (n.)," accessed May 27, 2022, https://www.merriam
-webster.com/dictionary/insanity.

7. *Narcotics Anonymous Basic Text*, 6th edition (Chatsworth, CA: Narcotics Anonymous World Services, Inc.), 23.

Chapter 2

1. "What Is a Substance Use Disorder?" American Psychiatric Association, accessed May 22, 2022, https://www.psychiatry.org/patients-families/addiction/what-is -addiction#:~:text=People%20with%20SUD%20have%20an,causing%20or%20 will%20cause%20problems.

2. "What Is a Substance Use Disorder?" American Psychiatric Association.

3. "Addictions," American Psychological Association, accessed May 22, 2022, https:// www.apa.org/topics/substance-use-abuse-addiction.

4. MedlinePlus, "Substance Use Recovery and Diet," National Library of Medicine, February 18, 2022, https://medlineplus.gov/ency/article/002149.htm.

5. Claire Twark, "Can Exercise Help Conquer Addiction?," Harvard Medical School, December 26, 2018, https://www.health.harvard.edu/blog/can-exercise -help-conquer-addiction-2018122615641.

6. "Drugs, Brain, and Behavior: The Science of Addiction—Treatment and Recovery," National Institute on Drug Abuse, accessed March 22, 2022, https://nida.nih .gov/publications/drugs-brains-behavior-science-addiction/treatment-recovery.

7. "Opioid Overdose Crisis," National Institute on Drug Abuse, accessed May 22, 2022, https://nida.nih.gov/drug-topics/opioids/opioid-overdose-crisis.

8. "Addictions," American Psychological Association.

9. Deborah S. Hasin, et al. "DSM-5 Criteria for Substance Use Disorders: Recommendations and Rationale." *The American Journal of Psychiatry* 170, no. 8 (2013): 834-51, doi:10.1176/appi.ajp.2013.12060782.

10. "Public Policy Statement: Definition of Addiction," American Society of Addiction Medicine, updated September 15, 2019, https://sitefinitystorage.blob.core .windows.net/sitefinity-production-blobs/b0209701-2099-441a-92c3-eb60c4a387 cb?sfvrsn=a8f64512_0.

11. "Definition of Addiction," American Society of Addiction Medicine.

12. "Is A.A. for You?: Twelve Questions Only You Can Answer," Alcoholics Anonymous, accessed September 14, 2022, https://www.aa.org/sites/default/files /literature/assets/p-3_isaaforyou.pdf.

13. E. M. Jellinek, *The Disease Concept of Alcoholism*, (Eastford, CT: Martino Books, 1960).

14. Judit H. Ward et al., "Re-Introducing Bunky at 125: E. M. Jellinek's Life and Contributions to Alcohol Studies," *Journal of Studies on Alcohol and Drugs*, 77 no. 3 (May 2016): 381, https://www.jsad.com/doi/pdf/10.15288/jsad.2016.77.375.

15. Ward, "Re-Introducing Bunky at 125."

16. Ward, "Re-Introducing Bunky at 125."

17. Ward, "Re-Introducing Bunky at 125."

18. Ward, "Re-Introducing Bunky at 125."

19. "Human Services," Palm Beach State College, accessed May 22, 2022, https:// www.palmbeachstate.edu/career-pathways/pathway-education/default.aspx#ccc.

20. "Alcohol," World Health Organization, accessed March 15, 2022, https://www .who.int/health-topics/alcohol#tab=tab_1.

21. "Overdose Death Rates," Research Topics, National Institute on Drug Abuse, last revised January 20, 2022, www.drugabuse.gov/related-topics/trends-statistics/overdose-death-rates.
22. "Obesity," World Health Organization, June 9, 2021, https://www.who.int/news-room/facts-in-pictures/detail/6-facts-on-obesity.
23. "Diseases and Death," Centers for Disease Control and Prevention, page last reviewed June 2, 2021, https://www.cdc.gov/tobacco/data_statistics/fact_sheets/fast_facts/index.htm.
24. "Heroin Overdose Data," Centers for Disease Control and Prevention, last reviewed June 6, 2022, https://www.cdc.gov/drugoverdose/deaths/heroin/index.html.
25. "Drug Overdose Deaths in the U.S. Top 100,000 Annually," National Center for Health Statistics, Centers for Disease Control and Prevention, last reviewed November 17, 2021, https://www.cdc.gov/nchs/pressroom/nchs_press_releases/2021/20211117.htm.
26. "Facts About Fentanyl," United States Drug Enforcement Administration, accessed March 14, 2022, https://www.dea.gov/resources/facts-about-fentanyl.
27. Christina Echegaray, "Early Discharge of NAS Infants Prolongs Treatment," The Center for Child Health Policy, Vanderbilt University Medical Center, September 25, 2018, https://www.vumc.org/childhealthpolicy/news-events/early-discharge-nas-infants-prolongs-treatment.
28. James Olds and Peter Milner, "Positive Reinforcement Produced by Electrical Stimulation of Septal Area and Other Regions of Rat Brain," *Journal of Comparative Psychology* 47, no. 6 (1954): 419–27, http://dx.doi.org/10.1037/h0058775.
29. Morten L. Kringlebach and Kent C. Berridge, "The Functional Neuroanatomy of Pleasure and Happiness," *Discovery Medicine* 9, no. 49 (June 2010), https://www.ncbi.nlm.nih.gov/pmc/articles/PMC3008353/#R33.

Chapter 3

1. Christopher Wanjek, "Controlled Drinking: Controversial Alternative to AA," LiveScience, December 4, 2007, www.livescience.com/2065-controlled-drinking-controversial-alternative-aa.html.
2. "Benzodiazepines," Alcohol and Drug Foundation, August 26, 2022, https://adf.org.au/drug-facts/benzodiazepines/.
3. Deborah Sontag, "Addiction Treatment with a Dark Side," *New York Times*, November 16, 2013, https://www.nytimes.com/2013/11/17/health/in-demand-in-clinics-and-on-the-street-bupe-can-be-savior-or-menace.html?searchResultPosition=1.
4. "Drugs and Supplements: Naltrexone (Oral Route)," Mayo Clinic, accessed May 22, 2022, https://www.mayoclinic.org/drugs-supplements/naltrexone-oral-route/precautions/drg-20068408.
5. NIDA, "Drugs, Brains, and Behavior: The Science of Addiction," National Institute on Drug Abuse, updated July 2020, https://nida.nih.gov/publications/drugs-brains-behavior-science-addiction/treatment-recovery; Anna Ciulla, "You're

in Recovery. What Should You Eat?" *U.S. News & World Report*, December 3, 2018, https://health.usnews.com/health-care/for-better/articles/2018-12-03/foods -that-are-good-for-addiction-recovery/; Marc Lewis, "Addiction and the Brain: Development, Not Disease," *Neuroethics* 10 no. 1 (January 2017): 7–18, https:// doi.org/10.1007/s12152-016-9293-4.

6. Marc Lewis, "Addiction and the Brain."

7. Shadia Kawa and James Giordano, "A Brief Historicity of the *Diagnostic and Statistical Manual of Mental Disorders*: Issues and Implications for the Future of Psychiatric Canon and Practice," *The Journal of Philosophy, Ethics, and Humanities in Medicine* 7 no. 2, published online January 13, 2012, https://www.ncbi.nlm .nih.gov/pmc/articles/PMC3282636/.

8. Nancy McWilliams, *Psychoanalytic Diagnosis* (New York: Guilford Press, 2011), 10.

9. Krutika Chokhawala and Lee Stevens, "Antipsychotic Medications," StatPearls, National Library of Medicine, updated March 8, 2022, https://www.ncbi.nlm .nih.gov/books/NBK519503/.

10. Partnership staff, "Adderall Abuse Increases among High School Student," Partnership to End Addiction, December 2013, https://drugfree.org/newsroom /news-item/adderall-abuse-increases-among-high-school-students/.

11. ADDitude editors, "Is it Safe to Medicate Our Child With ADHD?" *ADDitude: Inside the ADHD Mind*, September 16, 2021, https://www.additudemag.com/ slideshows/what are the side-effects-of-adhd-medication-on-kids/.

12. E. Derbyshire, "Do Omega-3/6 Fatty Acids Have a Therapeutic Role in Children and Young People with ADHD?" *Journal of Lipids* vol. 2017 (2017): 6285218, https://www.ncbi.nlm.nih.gov/pmc/articles/PMC5603098/.

13. NCPOEP, "Medication-Assisted Treatment (MAT) in Pregnancy—Overview," North Carolina Pregnancy & Opioid Exposure Project, accessed May 22, 2022, https://ncpoep.org/guidance-document/north-carolina-guidelines-medication -assisted-treatment-mat-in-pregnancy/mat-in-pregnancy/.

14. Arthur Robin Williams, "Pros and Cons of Medication-Assisted Treatment for Opioid Use Disorder," *Psychiatric Times*, July 12, 2018, https://www.psychiatrictimes .com/view/pros-and-cons-medication-assisted-treatment-opioid-use-disorder.

15. "Marijuana Education," Florida A & M University Medical Marijuana Education and Research Initiative, accessed May 24, 2022, https://mmeri.famu.edu /educate?utm_source=iheartdigital&utm_medium=googleads.

16. Marc Freeman, "More Arrests to Come in Crackdown on Drug-Recovery Industry, Prosecutor Vows," *South Florida Sun Sentinel*, January 13, 2022, https://www .sun-sentinel.com/local/palm-beach/fl-nc-palm-beach-sober-homes-prosecution -update-20200113-ires7jxjgnfczayoj2ysqb4sru-story.html.

17. "Is Drug Addiction Treatment Worth Its Cost?" National Institute on Drug Abuse, *Principles of Drug Addiction Treatment: A Research-Based Guide*, 3rd ed., January 2018, https://nida.nih.gov/publications/principles-drug-addiction-treat ment-research-based-guide-third-edition/frequently-asked-questions/drug -addiction-treatment-worth-its-cost.

18. "The U.S. Addiction Rehab Industry," Market Research.com, January 2020, https://www.marketresearch.com/Marketdata-Enterprises-Inc-v416/Addiction

-Rehab-12943155/?progid=91619&hsCtaTracking=c575b337-72bb-4d3a-ac1c
-6eca4e65d4d6%7C6e35b7a2-d103-4fff-8e74-e885b52c67be.

19. Rajita Sinha, "New Findings on Biological Factors Predicting Addiction Relapse Vulnerability," *Current Psychiatry Reports* 13, no. 398 (October 2011), https://doi .org/10.1007%2Fs11920-011-0224-0.

20. *Alcoholics Anonymous Big Book*, 4th ed. (New York: Alcoholics Anonymous World Services, 2001), xxix.

21. Alexandre B. Laudet, Keith Morgen, and William L. White, "The Role of Social Supports, Spirituality, Religiousness, Life Meaning and Affiliation with 12-Step Fellowships in Quality of Life Satisfaction among Individuals in Recovery from Alcohol and Drug Problems," *Alcoholism Treatment Quarterly* 24, no. 1–2 (2006), https://doi.org/10.1300%2FJ020v24n01_04.

22. *Alcoholics Anonymous Big Book*, 4th ed. (New York: Alcoholics Anonymous World Services, 2001), xx. aa.org/the-big-book.

23. Deena McMahon, "When Trauma Slips into Addiction," *The Imprint Youth and Family News*, December 17, 2018, https://imprintnews.org/child-trauma-2 /when-trauma-slips-into-addiction/32462.

24. "Cannabis (Marijuana) Research Report: Is There A Link Between Marijuana Use and Psychiatric Disorders?" *National Institute on Drug Abuse*, April 13, 2021, https://nida.nih.gov/publications/research-reports/marijuana/there-link -between-marijuana-use-psychiatric-disorders.

Chapter 4

1. Rajita Sinha, "New Findings on Biological Factors Predicting Addiction Relapse Vulnerability," *Current Psychiatry Reports* 13, no. 398 (October 2011), https://doi .org/10.1007%2Fs11920-011-0224-0.

2. Mandy Erickson, "Alcoholics Anonymous Most Effective Path to Alcohol Abstinence," *Stanford Medicine*, News, March 11, 2020, https://med.stanford.edu/news /all-news/2020/03/alcoholics-anonymous-most-effective-path-to-alcohol -abstinence.html.

3. "Researchers Identify Alcoholism Subtypes," National Institutes of Health news release, June 28, 2007, www.nih.gov/news-events/news-releases/researchers -identify-alcoholism-subtypes.

Chapter 6

1. Bruce K. Alexander, "Addiction: The View from Rat Park," 2010, www.bruce kalexander.com/articles-speeches/rat-park/148-addiction-the-view-from-rat-park.

2. Karen J. Mathewson, Cheryl H. T. Chow, Kathleen G. Dobson, Eliza I. Pope, Louis A. Scmidt, and Ryan J. Van Lieshout, "Mental Health of Extremely Low Birth Weight Survivors: A Systematic Review and Meta-Analysis," *Psychological Bulletin* 143, no. 4 (2017): 347–383, https://www.apa.org/pubs/journals/releases /bul-bul0000091.pdf.

3. British Neuroscience Association, "Fetal Exposure to Excessive Stress Hormones in the Womb Linked to Adult Mood Disorders," *ScienceDaily*, April 7, 2013, https://www.sciencedaily.com/releases/2013/04/130407090835.htm.

4. Ed Henry, *42 Faith: The Rest of the Jackie Robinson Story* (Nashville: Thomas Nelson, 2017), 60–61.

5. Stewart D. Friedman, "How Our Careers Affect Our Children," *Harvard Business Review*, November 14, 2018, https://hbr.org/2018/11/how-our-careers-affect-our-children.

6. Dulce Gonzalez, Arian Bethencourt Mirabal, Janelle D. McCall, "Child Abuse and Neglect," StatPearls (January 2022), https://www.ncbi.nlm.nih.gov/books/NBK459146/.

Part 3

1. *Merriam-Webster*, s.v. "cure (n.)," accessed September 15, 2019, https://www.merriam-webster.com/dictionary/cure.

Chapter 10

1. *A Course in Miracles: Based On the Original Handwritten Notes of Helen Schucman—Complete & Annotated Edition* (Sedona, AZ: Circle of Atonement, Inc., 2017), xxxv, paragraph 2.

2. *A Course in Miracles*, xxxv, paragraph 3.

Chapter 11

1. Kahlil Gibran, *The Prophet* (New York: Penguin Books, 2019), 58.

2. Lana Burgess, "Eight Benefits of Crying: Why It's Good to Shed a Few Tears," *MedicalNewsToday*, October 7, 2017, https://www.medicalnewstoday.com/articles/319631#benefits-of-crying.

Chapter 12

1. *A Course in Miracles* (Mill Valley, CA: Foundation for Inner Peace, 1976), 214.

2. *A Course in Miracles*, 402.

3. *A Course in Miracles*, 367.

Chapter 14

1. *A Course in Miracles* (Mill Valley, CA: Foundation for Inner Peace, 1976), 255.

FREE BONUS

Would you like more information on healing addiction? Do you have trouble accessing your feelings? Find a free meditation to help with this along with many helpful tools on various platforms. Checkout the You-Tube channel Dr. Donna Marks for videos on addiction, mediations, and her *A Course in Miracles* classes. Want more than a book? You can check out her *Exit the Maze* podcast and online group discussions at DrDonnaMarks .com to help accelerate your healing process. For more information and to access this bonus and videos, please visit DrDonnaMarks.com.